from
DREAMING
to
BECOMING

xulon
PRESS

Praise for *From Dreaming to Becoming* by Phinehas Kinuthia

"This exceptional work by Phinehas Kinuthia is one of the most profound, practical, principle-centered approaches to the subject on fulfilling your dreams I have read in a long time. The author's approach to this timely and critical issue of leadership brings a fresh breath of air that captivates the heart, engages the mind and inspires the spirit of the reader. *From Dreaming to Becoming* is destined to become a classic and touch many lives."

Dr. Myles Munroe
BFMI International
Nassau Bahamas

"Phinehas Kinuthia has written a fantastic book on how to see the dream that God has given you come true. He takes you through an entire process that if followed will get you well on your way to seeing that dream be a reality. Most of us have dreams; we simply don't know what to do with them. I whole heartedly encourage everyone to read this book."

Bob Roberts Jr.
Senior Pastor NorthWood Church
Author, *Bold as Love*
Twitter; @bobrobertsjr blog; www.glocal.net

"Watch when the future homeowners sit with the architect. They twist and articulate their bodies for emphasis, punctuate the air with their fingers to describe, and draw vertical lines with their hands lifted high to try to accentuate the house they see in their dreams. It is in their minds, it is in their heads, but the builder must have it on paper. It takes a good architect to listen closely and employ his or her skill set to take the mind's castle and develop it into the home of their dreams. Before there is a becoming, there must be a dreaming. To move from dreaming to reality, there must be a becoming. All great things began with a dream and start with a concept, but many of us get mired in the morass between the thought and the action. Phinehas Kinuthia has drawn a mind map to take each reader from concept to product, from thoughts to realities, from wispy, ethereal mind games to concrete realities where real progress is made. I recommend you sit with this mind architect and let him step you through the process of building the 'house of your dreams.' And when you are done reading this choice book, you will be able to say, 'I have gone from dreaming to becoming.'"

Pastor Brett Jones
Senior Pastor Grace Church Humble

"*From Dreaming to Becoming* by Phinehas Kinutha is a much needed book today. So many people have dreams that follow them to the grave. Phinehas provides the principle that moves one from imagination to manifestation. *From Dreaming to Becoming* is practical, principled, and purposefully written so that the reader can anticipate Becoming. I am thankful that Phinehas's dream of helping others with their dreams is now a reality."

Dr. John D. Ogletree Jr.
Senior Pastor, First Metropolitan Church
Houston, Texas

"Phinehas Kinuthia has carefully laid out a plan for success. His insights have been proven to be the result of much study, living through struggle, and never giving up on his dreams. It would be worthwhile to any reader to study this work and to keep it close for inspiration, information, and motivation to keep your own dreams alive. I would recommend that this be a gift book to give to all your friends."

Anthony Fouts
Director of Church Growth Solutions

"This is not a book but a blueprint on how to live your life! With every page filled to the brim with wisdom, knowledge, and encouragement, I would highly recommend this to anyone who is trying to chase an 'impossible' dream. This book will show you how to make the impossible dream possible by giving you the steps you need to get out of the muck and mire of your day-to-day, nine-tofive job and put you on the mountain top of success!"

Harold
MyMorningJoe.com

"In his inaugural book, Phinehas Kinuthia recasts the necessity of converting our potential energy into kinetic energy. Our greatest value is not in acknowledged potential, but its transformation from an unseen existence to a visible, tangible reality. Phinehas shares these ten poignant, proven, and achievable principles in the context of past and present successes as a testament to the rich future available from their adherence. These are ten simple principles for dream realization. As a Professor of Physics, I have noted over the past ten years that I am not only a purveyor of information but also of values. Students many times prior to acting must know that their dreams of passing my course or attaining their degrees is possible. Therefore, I employ several of the principles that Phinehas shares in this book, and I know from anecdotal and evaluative experience they work! Eloquently written, *From Dreaming to Becoming* is the fruit of Phinehas living what he has written; this will undoubtedly enrich everyone who not only reads the contents of this monograph but dares to live the principles found herein."

Kevin Storr, Ph.D.
Associate Professor of Physics
Prairie View A & M University

"As a college administrator in one of the most diverse cities in the country, I interact with thousands of young people, many of whom come to the United States looking for greater opportunity for themselves and their families. One of those people I encountered was Phinehas Kinuthia. While many have a dream and are searching for opportunities, I find that relatively few have a clear vision how to reach their dream—Phinehas does. This book articulates what I have already witnessed about Phinehas. He does not sit back waiting to be empowered by others, nor does he feel entitled to anything for that which he is not willing to work. I especially appreciate the attitude as expressed in the book that there is no one to blame besides yourself should you fall short of achieving a goal. Preparation and hard work, as Phinehas calls "the principles of perspiration," are proven formulas for success—although a measure of luck doesn't hurt either!"

Claire Phillips, PhD
Instructional Dean Math, Sciences, and Engineering

"From his difficult childhood in Africa to his congregational success in the United States, Phinehas Kinuthia has pursued his dream of becoming an inspirational teacher and leader. In this informative and instructive book, he tells us how to own and pursue our dreams with focus. Phinehas has much to say, and I found myself listening carefully."

Susan L. Yarbrough
Former Judge

"Dreams are the vehicle God gives us to make our lives fulfilling and make a difference in the lives of others and our communities. In this book you will be inspired by Phinehas Kinuthias's practical and transcending tools encouraging you to pursue the dream within you."

Susan Nichols
Community Developer

from DREAMING *to* BECOMING

10 Essential Principles for Living the Life of Your Dreams

By
Phinehas Kinuthia

Copyright © 2013 by Phinehas Kinuthia

FROM DREAMING TO BECOMING
by Phinehas Kinuthia

Printed in the United States of America

ISBN 9781625097453

All rights reserved solely by the author. The author guarantees all contents are original and do not infringe upon the legal rights of any other person or work. No part of this book may be reproduced in any form without the permission of the author. The views expressed in this book are not necessarily those of the publisher.

Unless otherwise noted, all Scripture quotations are taken from the King James Version of the Bible. (Public Domain.) Scripture quotations marked NIV are taken from the Holy Bible, New International Version®, NIV®. Copyright © 1973, 1978, 1984 by Biblica, Inc™. Used by permission of Zondervan. All rights reserved worldwide. www.zondervan.com; CEV are taken from the *Contemporary English Version* © 1995 by American Bible Society. Used by permission; NKJV are taken from the New King James Version. Copyright © 1982 by Thomas Nelson, Inc. Used by permission. All rights reserved.

www.xulonpress.com

Dedication

This book is dedicated to my wife, Joyce, and our daughter, Claire. Without you, my dreams are incomplete. Thank you for the sacrifices you have made, believing in me, and encouraging me to pursue my dream.

To my father and mother, Peter and Nelly Kinuthia, to my brother, Charles, my sister, Naomi, thank you for the values and courage you instilled in me. Thank you for your faith in me, your belief in my dreams, and for being selfless with your resources, time, and love. You believed in me and have always seen more in me than I saw in myself. I can never ask for a better family than you.

To all the dreamers who at some point lost hope in their dreams, may the hope enveloped in this message birth a relentless desire to be more than you have ever been. It is possible and it's never too late to become what you have always imagined.

Acknowledgements

To God, who is the Giver and the Fulfiller of all dreams.

To all my mentors and life coaches whose lives have personally impacted me through direct or indirect influence through media, books, and involvement in my life, I am exceedingly thankful. Your accomplishments and love for humanity and its advancement has inspired me.

To my friends and everyone who made this project a reality, you are exceptional. Thank you for the encouragement and support. I am forever grateful.

To my executive administrator, Nancy, who labored so hard to ensure the completion of this project.

Contents

Introduction 19

Chapter 1: The Principle of Purpose 29
Chapter 2: The Principle of Perception 44
Chapter 3: The Principle of Associations 57
Chapter 4: The Principle of Ownership 67
Chapter 5: The Principle of Preparation 89
Chapter 6: The Principle of Perspiration 104
Chapter 7: The Principle of Tradeoffs 115
Chapter 8: The Principle of Assessment 132
Chapter 9: The Principle of Faith 142
Chapter 10: The Principle of Passion 154
Conclusion 161

Notes 163
About the Author 167

Introduction

Inside each of us is a dream. Many dreams haven't been realized, remaining in the imaginations of many great men and women. Countless victories are unclaimed and success stories are waiting to be told. Many people will live and die without accomplishing their dreams or becoming what they were intended to be. Several who have envisioned a dream are devastated to see it realized by someone else. Perhaps you are like me and for a long time have had a dream but never knew how to bring it to life. Most of us are frustrated by our inability to accomplish our dreams.

Despite our respective social economical backgrounds or status in life, we all have dreams that developed in our childhoods. Everyone dreams of becoming successful or achieving something significant in life. For many years I dreamed about making a difference in other people's life, becoming a published author, being debt free, quitting my job to start my own organization. But these dreams never moved beyond thoughts and occasionally updating my goals on paper. I lived a life of mediocrity, wishing and praying that my life would be different. It wasn't until I learned and then embraced these ten essential principles that I began living the life of my dreams. Our greatest challenge is taking our dreams from thoughts and wishes and making them realities.

From Dreaming to Becoming is not a rags to riches story, yet if you follow these ten principles, you are likely to attain significant accomplishments that will yield financial reward. My goal is to help you learn and apply these principles so that you can set your dreams in motion. I do not profess to have all the solutions or to be the final authority on this subject, because one book cannot resolve everything; however, my goal with this book is to equip you with the blueprints, tools, and effective principles that have worked to make some of my dreams come true. *From Dreaming to Becoming* contains life lessons that I have distilled from my own journey in pursuit of my dreams. These ten proven principles are guaranteed to work in your life to make everything you've ever dreamed of become a reality. In the words of Carl Mays, "The real challenge and the real reward is to take who you are and what you are capable of doing, and create the means to achieve your dreams."[1]

Dreamers are pioneers. They are world changers and pacesetters who leave footprints of their successes. True dreamers not only dream but become what or who they

INTRODUCTION

dreamed of doing or being. True dreamers determine and chart the course of their lives. Some have fulfilled their biggest dreams and have effected great changes in how the world operates today, from the way we store food, travel to work, transact business, and communicate with loved ones. Their realized dreams have defined the realities of our lives by changing our world. Andy Stanley in *Visioneering* talks about how the Wright brothers' dreams secured their place in history:

> On December 17, 1903, at 10:35 a.m., Orville Wright secured his place in history by executing the first powered and sustained flight from level ground. For twelve gravity-defying seconds he flew for 120 feet along the dunes of the outer banks of North Carolina. In the field of aviation, his historic event represents a beginning. But for Orville and Wilbur Wright, it was the end of a long and tedious journey. A journey initiated by a dream common to every little boy—the desire to fly. But what most children abandon to the domain of fantasy, Orville and Wilbur Wright seized upon as potential reality. They believed they could fly.[2]

From Dreaming to Becoming

Dreams Add Flight to Your Life

The Wright brothers had a dream of flying; that dream has created and defined worldwide air transportation commerce.

Fred Smith, founder of FedEx, had a dream of creating an express delivery system, an idea he proposed in a college paper. His professor frowned upon the idea and consequently gave Smith a C on his paper. However, today we cannot imagine a world without FedEx or other overnight couriers. Fred Smith's dream now defines how business is done in an entire industry.

Probably one of the greatest examples we have today of a true dreamer is Dr. Martin Luther King Jr. in what was birthed and reverberated through time from the steps of the Lincoln Memorial on August 28, 1963, the famous "I have a dream" speech. Today we enjoy the impact of a man who dared to dream about fighting injustice and reconciling a nation to work together irrespective of color. While we who live after this great man's death continue his legacy, his dream became a defining moment for the civil rights movement.

I could not agree more with what the builders of the magnificent Seville Cathedral said, "Let us build here a church so great that those who come after us will think us mad to have ever dreamed of it!" The Colosseum in Rome, the Taj Mahal in India, the Golden Gate Bridge were first dreams in someone's mind before they became the wonders of the world. One man's dream can have great implication. One woman's dream can change the world. If you and I dare to dream, we can revolutionize the world—if not the whole world, at least the private worlds we live daily.

> *All men who have achieved great things have been great dreamers.*
> Orison Swett Marden

As you read *From Dreaming to Becoming*, you may have lost hope in your dream. Maybe the recent global financial crises may have annihilated your great hopes for attaining your dreams. Maybe you are a foreigner living in another country, feeling lost and insignificant, and you have lost even the potential to dream because life in your new country is not what you expected it to be. I know what that's like because I have been where you are. Maybe you have lost your identity and cannot believe in your dreams because life's struggles are too many and they feel too difficult to overcome. Perhaps, you are contemplating throwing in the towel because you have lost your family, your job, your investments, and now your dreams have dried up and are gone with the winds of struggle. I'm here to say that you can dream again.

From Dreaming to Becoming

Do you believe your dream is too big and unattainable? Are you sick enough of how things have been that you desire change, yet you are clueless as to how to accomplish your dream? By reading *From Dreaming to Becoming* you've already taken your first step to attaining your dream. These ten principles will teach you how to execute your dream and ideas, how to move from one point to the next. Applying these principles will help you begin and follow through on the exciting journey of fulfilling your dreams. You have to be willing to challenge yourself to let go of a faulty past belief system or the idea that you know it all, and instead embrace these new principles and new ideas. They have changed my life and I know they will change your life.

Grab Your Dream and Don't Let Go

Dreamers don't lose sight of their dreams. They fight to hold on to their dreams and know that although their dreams may tarry, they will come to pass if they are pursued. Oftentimes the dream seems impossible, outlandish, or even fanciful, but don't lose sight of your dream. Do not let people talk you out of your dream. Don't stop believing in your dream. Don't give up on your dream. If others killed your dream because they laughed at it, told you it was ridiculous or pie-in-the-sky, or looked at you like you were crazy, I encourage you to recapture your dream. Great things happen when we relentlessly pursue our dreams. Your dream might be in music, sports, arts or science, medicine, engineering, ministry, politics, law, multiple fields of ingenuity, or maybe it's simply to travel to exotic locations, learn how to dance, learn a new language, or simply meet new friends. Perhaps your dream is to be debt free or develop financial security and give to the poor, or even to add value in the lives of others and make a difference in the world. You are not too old to pursue the dream that's in your heart.

> **Your casket is too small to carry you and your dream when you die. Don't die with unrealized dreams.**

Dr. Myles Munroe, a leadership and motivation expert, believes that the wealthiest place on earth is not the banks but in the cemeteries, where great untapped resources lie six feet beneath the surface. This wealth could be unwritten books, business ideas, inventions, formulas, philosophies, and innovations that lie unexcavated, hidden in unfulfilled dreams. Your casket is too small to carry you and your dream when you die. Don't die with unrealized dreams. No matter how young or old you are, your dream is what the world is missing today. I wrote *From Dreaming to Becoming* with you in mind, and by the time you finish reading this book, my hope is that you will conceive a belief system that moves you from dreaming to becoming, so that you will start living the life of your dreams.

> *If you can dream it, you can do it.*
> Walt Disney

Got Dreams?

A dream is a dominant idea that is ever present within us and constantly provokes us to greatness and awakens a desire to want to do all that we can to be more than we are. A true dream is not idle thoughts; nor is it temporary fascinations or infatuations.

A dream is God's blueprint regarding your potential future. It is a definite mental picture of your future. It is meant to inspire hope and birth expectation, which motivates action toward what could be rather than what is.

Perhaps we will find inspiration in experts' definitions of a dream.

- Business consultant Robert Kriegel says that "A dream is an ideal involving a sense of possibilities rather than probabilities, of potential rather than limits. A dream is the wellspring of passion, giving us direction and pointing us to lofty

heights. It is an expression of optimism, hope and values lofty enough to capture the imagination and engage the spirit. Dreams grab us and move us. They are capable of lifting us to new heights and overcoming self-imposed limitations."[3]
- "Dreams are today's answers to tomorrow's questions." Edgar Cayce
- "Dreams are the children of your soul, the blueprints of your ultimate achievements." Napoleon Hill
- "A dream is a better future in need of an architect who will show others how to make it a reality." Ed Rowell

Having a dream will feed your expectations of the future, which in turn generates the ability to birth your dream in the present. The dream you nurture or build upon today is what you become tomorrow.

Having a dream is the fuel to the soul of your destiny. When you fuel your dream, you fuel your future. A dream will accelerate the latent potential lying dormant in you; it will stir up your gift. Without a dream your future looks insignificant and your reason for being seems irrelevant. A life without a dream is like a ship without a course. It lingers within the vicinity of the shores and never explores the splendor, beauty, and riches of the deep seas.

From Dreaming to Becoming

A dream is so vital to life that God promised that in the last days he would "Pour out his Spirit upon all people and the old men would dream dreams and young men would see visions."[4] True dreamers not only visualize their dreams but seek to actualize their dreams. Perhaps you have heard of or studied Maslow's hierarchy of needs. He states that humans' ultimate need is self-actualization and self-fulfillment. *From Dreaming to Becoming* will equip you with tools for actualizing your dream. My goal throughout the chapters in this book is to help you be all that you were intended to be. Bruce Springsteen said, "There comes a time when you need to stop waiting for the man you want to become and to start being the man you want to be."

> **A dream is a dominant idea that is ever present within us. It constantly provokes us to greatness and awakens a desire to do all that we can to be more than we are.**

I believe that your time has come to start living your bold dreams. In the words of Jim Rohn, international author and America's leading business authority on success, "The greatest value is not what we acquire; rather the greatest value is what we become."

Are you ready to become?

Chapter 1

THE PRINCIPLE OF PURPOSE

You must build your dreams around your purpose and your gifts in life.

Recently I read an interesting article on Today.com of a sheep named Jack that belongs to Alison and Simon, who own a farm in Shropshire, England. What struck me is that when Jack was a newborn, they brought him indoors because he was small. Since then, they have raised him together with their dog, Jessie, a springer spaniel. Jack thinks he is a dog. He fetches sticks, walks on a leash, and even tries to bark like a dog. When Jack is put with his flock, he tries to herd the other sheep.

Many people today live like Jack. We try to bark when we were born to bleat, and no matter how hard we work to perfect our "barking" or convince ourselves it's a "woof," it will always be a "baa." The truth is Jack the sheep will never be Jessie the dog because he was never born to be a dog.

    I found out long ago that if I was going to move from dreaming to becoming, I had to understand who or what I was born to be. A lizard can never be an alligator. It does not matter what geographical location you put a lizard—whether in Africa or the United States—a lizard will still be a lizard. You and I will never be successful in being what we were never born to be. Most people get frustrated because they try too hard to be what they were never equipped to be. In his classic book *Think and Grow Rich*, Napoleon Hill states, "There is one quality which one must possess to win and that is definiteness of purpose, the knowledge of what one wants and a burning desire to possess it."[1]

> You and I will never be fully successful in being what we were never born to be.

    Your mother or father probably told you that you could be anything you want to be if you put your mind to it. I don't want to be the bearer of bad news, but in your opinion do you think Jack can be a dog if he puts his mind to it? I would love to be a professional basketball player or football player, but I am not built for it. I am not six feet tall or cut out to compete as a linebacker

THE PRINCIPLE OF PURPOSE

in football. Some will argue that I can train hard enough to be anything I want to be. This is true, but too many of us have given up our perfect, intended selves to become a cheap imitation of others—and yet without any fulfillment. Who is the real you that has never existed in the world that you have created?

When you know who you are, you won't try to be what you were not meant to be. You might be asking, "So how do I decide who I am meant to be, given the plethora of choices that are available?" The answer is simple: know your purpose. Lou Holtz, former head football coach of national champions Notre Dame, says that most people have trouble making decisions, but decisions are easy to make if you know what your purpose is. A great scripture in the Bible tells us, "The light of the body is the eye: therefore when thine eye is single, thy whole body also is full of light; but when thine eye is evil, thy body also is full of darkness."[2]

> *Success demands singleness of purpose.*
> Vince Lombardi

Your life should begin and end with purpose. Your dream needs to be tied to your purpose. So that raises the next question: what is purpose? Purpose is the product's original objective as intended by the manufacturer. It is the desired result; it is the why question of production.

Purpose is never independent of design. Each product has specifications that are meant to fulfill a certain objective. Purpose defines the intended plan of the thing; this is why we need to learn to propagate the purpose for which we were created, because this is the reason for our being.

> **The empowerment within you is proportionate to your assignment.**

Pursuing a dream for which you have no passion or gifts leads to frustration, this is why the masses of men lead lives of quiet desperation. A great pitcher must be able to pitch well, but he doesn't have to hit well. Frustration comes when we hire a great pitcher and try to force him to do the work of a great hitter. Your dream should bring you closer to who you were born to be. Every dream you have should be guided by your purpose in life. It is your purpose that determines whether you are a great pitcher or a great hitter. Your purpose defines your ability and uniquely defines your value. Remember, the empowerment within you is proportionate to your assignment in life.

God gave you talents and gifts to facilitate how you get your assignment in life accomplished. When God puts a gift in you, He creates a need for the gift, and whenever your gift satisfies that need, you have found your calling, your purpose. Therefore, discover your purpose; the discovery and pursuit of your purpose is half the process of attaining it.

I recommend that you read the book *Living Your Strengths* by Albert L. Wiseman, Donald O. Clifton, and Curt Liesveld, which includes an ID code that gives you access to the Clifton Strengths Finder personality assessment online. This great tool will help you define your most dominant talents so you can build your life around your strengths and not focus on the distractions from your weaknesses.

> **Regardless of how successful you are, if you are not fulfilling your purpose, you will always have a sense of dissatisfaction.**

Your job is to discover and launch your uniqueness, which will make you indomitable. The Creator decides purpose, but the creation discovers. When you discover your purpose, you will automatically find fulfillment in life. Regardless of how successful you are, if you are not fulfilling your purpose, you will always have a sense of dissatisfaction.

Most people are dissatisfied because they are living outside of purpose and they don't realize it. They don't understand why they are unfulfilled, which leads to increased frustration. No matter how much money or

From Dreaming to Becoming

wealth you acquire, you will never be fulfilled unless you are fulfilling your purpose. We call this process fulfillment because you are fully accomplishing your assignment. As you advance in the direction of your dream, your dream should bring you closer to who you were born to be. Dr. Myles Munroe, said, "The only thing worse than death is a life without purpose. It is better to be dead and not worry about living than to live and not know why. Purpose is the key to life. Without purpose, life has no meaning."

I love this poem that echoes this sentiment

> There was a very cautious man,
> Who never laughed or played.
> He never risked, he never tried;
> He never sang or prayed.
> And when he one day passed away
> His insurance was denied.
> For since he never lived,
> They claimed he never died.
>
> Anonymous

Let us endeavor so to live that when we come to die even the undertaker will be sorry.

Mark Twain

THE PRINCIPLE OF PURPOSE

In *Tuesdays with Morrie*, Morrie converses with Mitch, "So many people walk around with a meaningless life. They seem half asleep even when they're busy doing things they think are important. This is because they're chasing the wrong things. The way you get meaning into your life is to devote yourself to loving others, devote yourself to your community around you and to devote yourself to creating something that gives you purpose and meaning."[3]

This is a resounding theme: you must find your purpose to find the meaning of your life, instead of chasing false and superficial dreams. Evaluate yourself and learn what portion of your life's energy is absorbed by a superficial dream rather than what is authentic to your God-given purpose. Stop chasing after treasure and find your purpose; finding your purpose secures your treasure.

Ask yourself these thought-provoking questions to jump-start your process of discovering your purpose.

1. Why are you here?
2. Who are you? What defines you?
3. What are your God-given abilities, talents, strengths, and skills?
4. What comes naturally to you?
5. What makes you different from others?

6. What one thing do you consistently and easily do well that impacts others around you?
7. What do you feel totally passionate about? What do you love to do?
8. What do you want to accomplish and to be remembered for? What is your life about?
9. What would your perfect life look like?
10. What brings fulfillment to you in your career, hobbies, or spiritual life?

Starting Point

I hate being lost and not knowing where I am going. Whenever my wife and I take a trip, I like to know our destination. Before I secured a GPS, I would go to MapQuest or Google and print out directions to our destination, or I would ask someone for specific instructions to get where I wanted to go. Similarly, when I go to a mall or other large facility, I visit the directory to establish where I am and, based on my purpose for being there, where I want to go. If you were to wear a blindfold in a mall you've never been in, do you think you could locate the store you want? Will random chance get you where you need to be? Your quest for purpose begins by finding out who you are. Start by asking, "Who am I, and where do I want to go?"

You must know where you are in life before you can determine which direction to go to fulfill your purpose. Before I tell you how to establish where you are, let me first say how *not* to. Don't compare yourself with other people because they may not be interested in the same things you are looking for or going where you want to go. And just because someone is heading in the same direction as you doesn't mean they are going to the same destination. I have learned not to evaluate myself by other people's success or how busy my life is, but by the accomplishment I have made relative to my intended purpose in life. Comparing yourself with others limits your ability to pursue and achieve everything God intends for you. Bob Buford expounds this more in his book *Halftime*: "What you do best for God will rise out of the core being he has created within you. In the Lord's parable of talents, we learn the wonderful message that we will be held accountable only for what we were given, not for what others might have or expect of us."[4]

In the next chapter I will share with you more on how to establish where you are by changing how you perceive your current starting point; this will help you avoid a faulty start.

We all have assignments in life that answer the why question of our existence. It is in finding the answer to this question that our life's journey begins. In the words of German philosopher Friedrich Nietzsche, "He who has a why to live for can bear with almost any how."

> **Because someone is heading in the same direction as you doesn't mean they are going to the same destination.**

In his book *Man's Search for Meaning*, Victor Frankl, a Holocaust survivor who endured unspeakable horrors in a Nazi death camp, wrote about survival. "What was really needed was a fundamental change in our attitude toward life. We had to learn ourselves, and furthermore, we had to teach the despairing men that it did not really matter what we expected from life but rather what life expected of us. Life ultimately means taking the responsibility to find the right answer to its problems and to fulfill the tasks which it constantly set for each individual. This task and therefore the meaning of life, differ from man to man."[5]

Each of us has a task for which we are uniquely designed. So learn not to allow people to live vicariously through you and tell you what they think you ought to be.

> *To be yourself in a world that is constantly trying to make you something else is the greatest accomplishment.*
>
> Ralph Waldo Emerson

Find Your Purpose

Find your purpose and build your dream around it. Spend your time learning and doing only that which adds and builds toward your ultimate purpose. Your purpose is great, so don't narrow it down to the mundane task of life. Many times we feel the pressure to do what other people expect us to do.

If you are a parent, stop directing your children to your own failed ambitions. Find out what your child is equipped to be and enable them to become the best at it. If they are not equipped to do it, it's because they were not meant to be it.

You will never experience greatness without a life of purpose. So find your purpose and begin to live in it. Unless you find your purpose, you are dead to that cause for which you were created. You will not begin to live until you find the purpose for which you exist. Purpose lives beyond your wishes, so don't live a wishful life; live a purposeful life.

From Dreaming to Becoming

The secret of success is constancy to purpose.

Benjamin Disraeli

When God called Jeremiah, He declared to him, "Before he formed him, he knew him and ordained him to be a prophet to the nations."[6] Every one of us has a unique calling, an "authentic self" that is idiosyncratic to our assignment in life. In his book *Reposition*, T. D. Jakes advises, "The first step in repositioning yourself is arming yourself with accurate analysis of your gifts and dedicating your efforts to cultivating the area of your gifting . . . You must have the courage and tenacity to see that abstract fantasy become concrete reality in your life."[7] This is also echoed by Dr. Phillip C. McGraw in *Self Matters*, in which he writes about finding your authentic self as the process of finding your purpose in life. "The authentic self is the *you* that can be found at the absolute core. It is the part of you that is not defined by your job, or your function, or your role. It is the composite of all your unique gifts, skills, abilities, interests, talents, insights, and wisdom. It is all your strengths and values that are uniquely yours and need expression, versus what you have been programmed to believe you are 'supposed' to be and do."[8]

You were created to stand out. You have been given a cause in this world to execute; this cause is the intended plan of your Maker. True success is not in what you accomplish; it is in doing what God created you to do. It is impossible to do everything people want you to do and still accomplish what God has called you to do. God will be most glorified in your life when you are living in purpose and fulfilling all that you were intended to be. You are a solution to someone's problem. You are necessary in someone's life. Someone's life will not begin until you show up, but you cannot show up until you are ready to showcase your authentic self.

> True success is not in what you accomplish; it is in doing what God created you to do.

Finding your authentic self begins with letting go of your old belief system, your personal predisposition regarding who you think you are not. I am convinced that the challenge in the pursuit of your dream is not in who you think you are that will limit you; rather, it's who you think you are not. I encourage you to take the limits of your life. Debunk your self-limiting perceptions. Whenever you intend to load a new operating system in an old system, you have to first uninstall the old version then install the new version. You have to remove all the "junk" you have been fed about yourself from others and start connecting with your authentic self.

DREAM AXIOMS

- Dreams add flight to your life.

- Your casket is too small to carry you and your dream when you die. Don't die with unrealized dreams.

- A dream is a dominant idea that is ever present within us. It constantly provokes us to greatness and awakens a desire to do all that we can to be more than we are.

- A dream is God's blueprint regarding your potential future. It is a definite mental picture of your future. It is meant to inspire hope and birth expectation, which motivates action toward what could be rather than what is.

- The dream you nurture or build upon today is what you become tomorrow.

- A dream is the fuel to the soul of your destiny. When you fuel your dream, you fuel your future.

- A life without a dream is like a ship without a course. It lingers within the vicinity of the shores and never explores the splendor beauty of the deep seas.

- True dreamers not only visualize their dreams but seek to actualize their dreams.

- Build your dreams around your purpose and your gifts.

- Pursuing a dream for which you have no passion and are not gifted for leads to frustration.

- The empowerment within you is proportionate to your assignment in life.

- The discovery and pursuit of your purpose is half the process of attaining it.

- Stop chasing after treasure and find your purpose; finding your purpose secures your treasure.

- You will never experience greatness without a life of purpose.

- Purpose lives beyond your wishes, so don't live a wishful life; live a purposeful life.

- True success is not in what you accomplish; it is in doing what God created you to do.

- It is impossible to do everything people want you to do and still accomplish what God has called you to do.

Chapter 2

THE PRINCIPLE OF PERCEPTION

There is nothing either good or bad, but thinking it makes it so.

Williams Shakespeare

Wat Traimit, Bangkok, is home to the largest Buddha statue. In 1957 this eleven-foot, five-ton clay statue had to be relocated to a new monastery. When the workers began to lower the statue into place using a crane, the ropes broke. The statue fell to the ground, breaking the clay. The workers were afraid and ran away, leaving the statue on the mud. They believed this was a bad omen because the statue was a precious religious symbol. Later that evening, it rained so hard that everyone thought it was because of the fallen statue. In the morning, the head temple monk, who had dreamed that the statute was divinely inspired, came to check on the Buddha image. To his surprise he discovered something unexpected when he inspected the crack in the clay. Under the clay covering the statute was pure gold. The statue that was worth thousands before it was moved was now worth millions. Thousands of people visit it each year.

Nothing is ever as it first appears. Sometimes what we see is not necessarily what really is. This plain statue had a low value until the hidden treasure beneath the clay was revealed. We all possess treasure hidden in ordinariness, only valuable when discovered.

> **We all possess treasure hidden in ordinariness, only valuable when discovered.**

"Perception is defined as the individual interpretation of events or situations based on personal beliefs, emotions and intellectual positioning."[1] You perceive what you want to perceive, and you believe what you want to believe about yourself. Whatever you label a thing is what it becomes to you. It is interesting that six city blocks worth of fog contains no more than approximately one glass of water. In other words, fog is a lot of smoke but little substance. What we perceive is not truly what exists in reality. Your image and your ability will be shaped by the environment you were

From Dreaming to Becoming

brought up in. Your self-perception is the foundation upon which your life is built. Most people view life from a myopic paradigm, limited to the scope of their own experiences, personal beliefs, and intellectual positioning. Because of how we see ourselves, we eventually become what we perceive. It's what many call a self-fulfilling prophecy. You cannot move from dreaming to becoming with a mind-set dominated by failure and impossibility.

> *"I can" is more important than "I.Q."*
> Clark Johnson

I used to be a very negative person. Most people who had an unfortunate or disadvantaged childhood might share a similar disposition. We tend to feel like someone owes us something; like our lives were cursed, and whatever circumstances we are in is the way life has to be. However, I discovered that I have to continually arm myself with a "Yes I Can" motto if I am to attain my dreams. Only I can alter my thinking. Let me ask you this: Can you see yourself living in your dream? Do you see the reality of living in your dreams? Have you ever heard the maxim "They can . . . because they think they can"? And in the words of King Solomon, the wisest man ever to live, "As a man thinks in his heart so is he."[2] It is unfortunate yet true that we reinforce naturally what we envision mentally about who we are. I believe that we are wired to go as far as we can see. This is why your perception of yourself is vital to the success of your accomplishments.

> *You become what you think about*
> *all day long.*
> Ralph Waldo Emerson

It is unfortunate yet true that we reinforce naturally what we envision mentally about who we are.

Take Charge of Your Thoughts

It is therefore clear that we need to take charge of our thoughts if we are to take charge of our dreams and ultimately our destiny. We tend to be afraid to take charge of our thoughts or to even imagine going beyond our present state. We are afraid to experiment using our thought process to dream what some might perceive as impossible. We set artificial levees that prevent the mind from being flooded with uncommon ideas and imaginations of our potential futures. Leadership expert John Maxwell affirms that "Imagination is the soil that brings dreams to life."[3] Your mind has limitless capacity so break the levees on your thought process and allow yourself to visualize endless possibilities. For example, a bully will always act in a manner to belittle others to attain a sense of superiority, because inherent in him is low self-esteem. So the bully will seek to dominate others to ascertain a false sense of power.

Benjamin Disraeli, former prime minister of Britain, said that we will never go higher than our thoughts. With your mind's eye, see yourself actualizing your dream. Know that your beliefs will become your realities. A negative mind will not generate a positive life. We express outwardly what is imbedded inside; our outer expression is an outcome of our inner perception of ourselves. Do not allow people's limiting belief to define who you are.

> **A negative mind will not generate a positive life.**

I learned to develop a compelling conviction and to always have confident expectations that my dream is possible. The Bible describes what our thought process should be like: "Whatever is true, whatever is noble, whatever is right, whatever is pure, whatever is lovely, whatever is admirable, if anything is excellent or praiseworthy, think about such things."[4]

Those who move from dreaming to becoming do not rely on people's opinions; they are independent of

The Principle of Perception

other's opinions. To be effective in life, I must distinguish between people's opinions of who I am and the facts of who I am. Most people today have a distorted perception of themselves, so what we see in them is not who they really are, but more like a mirage effect of themselves, resulting in skewed interpretations and responses influenced by negative experiences in their lives. If most people have a distorted perception of who they are, how would they possibly have a correct perception of you? Remember that your association matters and it will most likely influence your perception.

> **We express outwardly what is imbedded inside; our outer expression is an outcome of our inner perception of ourselves.**

Sir William James of Harvard said, "The greatest discovery of our times is that human beings by changing the inner aspects of their lives ultimately change the outer aspect of their lives." Dreamers see themselves differently; they have a unique portrait of themselves. Harness empowering beliefs that compliment your dream. I encourage you to get David J. Schwartz's *Magic of Thinking Big* and Ben Carson's *Think Big*, these two great resources will help you develop the right belief system.

There is a saying that "dreams are like paints of a great artist. Your dreams are your paints; the world is your canvas. Believing is the brush that converts your dreams into a masterpiece of reality." Behavior follows belief; therefore, we must learn to inventory our belief system and discard any limiting perceptions of ourselves. Every aspect of your life, such as the way you feel about yourself, the quality of your relationships, the career you pursue, or the dreams you accomplish will significantly be impacted by your perception. What do you believe concerning your ability to accomplish your dreams? Your success will be significantly determined by your perception. In the words of Henry Ford, "Whether you think you can, or you think you can't—you're right." Your future is in your heart. You only conquer in the physical what you have conquered in the mind. It's hard to be big when little has you. Your performance and behavior are directly related to your self-image and will not supersede it.

Self-concept influences personal performance.

Mohammed Ali once said, "A man is a reflection of his imagination." People's perceptions mirror the path they walk and the experiences of their lives; however, few manage to alter that inward reflection when they learn from their past. Self-concept influences personal performance. Our thoughts, attitudes, concepts, beliefs, and the principles by which we live are treasures we bring forth in our future. In the words of Andrew Carnegie, "The man who acquires the ability to take full possession of his own mind may take possession of anything else which he is justly entitled." The Bible admonishes that we are to carefully guard our thoughts because they are the source of true life.[5]

The Two Wells

Two wells nourish your mind, and you choose which well you will draw from as you live your life. One is the well of your past failures; the second is the well of possibility and right perception that says "Yes I Can." From which well are you drawing your source of true life?

Never say you can't, because *can* is inherent and engraved in you by your Maker. "I *can* do all things, through Christ who gives me strength."[6] Just because you have not discovered your potential does not mean that you don't have potential. Ignorance of your potential does not negate your potential. Just because the light switch is off doesn't mean there is no electricity. Turn on the switch!

James S. Hewett told a story that Leonardo da Vinci was working on a large canvas in his studio. For a while he worked at it, choosing the subject, planning the perspective, sketching the outline, applying his own natural genius. Then suddenly he ceased, the painting still unfinished, and summoning one of his students he invited him to complete the work. The student protested that he was unworthy and unable to complete the great painting the master had begun. But da Vinci silenced him with these words: "Will not what I have done inspire you to do your best?" Your perception will always influence your performance; however, you must be confident in who you are and have an understanding that just like da Vinci did with his student, God requires from you only what He has already equipped you for.

> God requires from you only what He has already equipped you for.

Twelve spies surveyed the land of Canaan before the Israelites set out to possess the city. Ten of the spies reported that the inhabitants were giants and that the spies felt like grasshoppers next to them. Two spies returned with a different report that claimed victory was indeed possible and probable against the giants. All twelve surveyed the same land and inhabitants but came back with opposite perceptions. The people latched on to the negative report, resulting in their wandering in the wilderness, homeless for forty years. Had they listened to the positive report, they would have successfully routed the "giants," set up housekeeping in the rich land, and began building wealth.

> **The "I can't" mentality is the greatest obstacle in actualizing your dream. Instead of replacing your dreams, replace your wrong perception.**

I choose to see myself today the way I want to be perceived when my dream is realized. Life is a self-fulfilling prophecy; you will always get what you expect. The thought and talk of failure establishes failure. Create the right perception of yourself by focusing on vocabulary that is positive and uplifting. Remember that your subconscious mind is downloading your self-image into your belief system. Your dream will not become a reality until you wrap your mind around a different thought process.

> *The only place where dreams become impossible is in your own thinking*
> Robert H. Schuller

Learn to nurture the right perception about yourself; it will give you hope to look forward to a compelling future. I choose to nurture the thought that my dream is a mental possibility waiting to be transformed into a physical reality. The truth is you can do and be more than what you do and who you are today. Remember that thought precedes action. Pessimism and despair have to be countered by optimism and hope. The "I can't" mentality is the greatest obstacle in actualizing your dream. Instead of replacing your dreams, replace your wrong perception. As a dreamer, the image you allow of yourself determines the feelings you create. Your self-worth is your price tag. Don't sell yourself cheap.

In his book *Psychology of Winning,* Denis Waitley offers relevant questions for self-appraisal. This is a great starting point to evaluate how our perceptions are being influenced.

What are my dominant fears?

1. What motivating effects do these fears have in my life?
2. What are my dominant desires?
3. Do I focus most of my attention and thought on the desires?
4. Do I focus on the rewards of success more than on the penalties?[7]

DREAM AXIOMS

- We all possess treasure hidden in ordinariness, only valuable when discovered.

- You cannot move from dreaming to becoming with a mind-set dominated by failure and impossibility.

- We need to take charge of our thoughts if we are to take charge of our dreams and ultimately our destiny.

- Your mind has limitless capacity, so break the levees on your thought process and allow yourself to visualize endless possibilities.

- We express outwardly what is imbedded inside; our outer expression is an outcome of our inner perception of ourselves.

- Your beliefs will become your realities.

- A negative mind will not generate a positive life.

- Dreamers see themselves differently; they have a unique portrait of themselves.

- Your performance and behavior are directly related to your self-image and will not supersede it.

- Self-concept influences personal performance.

From Dreaming to Becoming

- Ignorance of your potential does not negate your potential.

- God requires from you only what He has already equipped you for.

- Your subconscious mind is downloading your self-image into your belief system.

- Your dream will not become a reality until you wrap your mind around a different thought process.

- Your self-worth is your price tag. Don't sell yourself cheap.

- See yourself today the way you want to be perceived when your dream is realized.

Chapter 3

THE PRINCIPLE OF ASSOCIATIONS

Things that have a common quality ever quickly seek their kind.

Marcus Aurelius

The old adage states "Show me your friends and I will show you who you are." Perhaps you've also heard "Birds of a feather flock together." My experience has been that people around me can never advance me beyond their current position in life. I think this holds true for everyone because it is hard to give what you do not have.

Associations are important. They are like elevators: some take you up, while others take you down. I entitled this chapter "The Principle of Association" because we become a part of whom we associate with. I learned to associate with people who add value to

From Dreaming to Becoming

my life and avoid those who discourage and stifle my dreams. Finding the right people to include in your life begins by evicting the wrong ones. Choose whom you lose—those who discourage you in your pursuits—and whom you gain—those who encourage you.

> *Your friends will stretch your vision . . .*
> *or choke your dreams.*
>
> Unknown

You will get farther in life by avoiding people who are critical of your dreams and especially those who do not believe you can achieve your dreams. The truth is you will never please all your critics and you will never win their approval, so quit trying to convince them that you are right and that your dream will come to pass. We spend so much energy trying to please and prove our dreams to critics that we lose the energy needed to pursue our dreams. In the words of Ralph Waldo Emerson, "Whatever course you decide upon, there is always someone to tell you that you are wrong." Albert Einstein also said, "Great spirits have always encountered violent opposition from mediocre minds."

I make it a point to isolate myself from negative people. The absence of people who do not add value to your life does not take anything away from you. Surround yourself with positive people who light up your dream world, people who make your dream world less obscure. Remember that you are always moving in the direction of your associations. Those whom you listen to have influence over your life. So make sure your associates are eager to help you succeed.

> **You will not get anywhere if you are surrounded by people who inhibit forward movement.**

In your pursuit of fulfilling your dreams, you will encounter difficulties, which will tempt you to believe that your critics are right. To map out a course of action and follow it to its completion requires courage. I am reminded of what T. D. Jakes wrote in *Maximize the Moment*: "Too often our actions are dictated not by our own sense of purpose but by a misguided need to please. We want to make others happy and will do anything to win their approval. We care so much what others think that with every step we take, we look over to see if our move is making someone smile. If you want to maximize your life and fulfill the plan that God has for you, you must take control of your life."[1]

You will not get anywhere if you are surrounded by people who inhibit forward movement. Dreamers who move from dreaming to becoming do not rely on other's opinions; they are independent of people's ideas in pursuing their dream. "Jesus did not commit himself unto them, because he knew all men, and needed not that any should testify of man: for he knew what was in man."[2]

Establish Common Goals Relationships

You become part of what or whom you are around. Your associations will inevitably influence your perception. We live in a negative world, so we have to associate with positive people in order to make our dreams a reality. It is my experience that successful people spend time with other successful people. I am not surprised that two of the wealthiest people in the world, Bill Gates and Warren Buffet, are great friends.

> Life is full of people of mediocrity and people of excellence; choose whose influence you permit.

Life is full of people of mediocrity and those of excellence; therefore, choose whose influence you permit. Dreamers are fascinated with becoming exceptional; they are not content with mediocrity. It is clear that even though we have to cut the umbilical cord of toxic relationships that derail our progress, we need to introduce new relationships in which we share common

THE PRINCIPLE OF ASSOCIATIONS

goals. Significant success will come when you link with people of same mind-set.

Answer these questions to assess the value of your associations:

1. What are the relationships in my life, and how do they contribute toward my dream?
2. Who is allowed in my circle of friends?
3. Who listens to and influences my decisions?
4. Who is asking questions about my dreams and goals?
5. Who expresses confidence in my dreams?
6. Who are the mentors and the circle of counsel in my life?
7. Do I have a dream team?
8. Who has accomplished what I want to accomplish, and what quality of people do they rally around them?
9. What biographies of uncommon achievers do I need to study?

There is a saying that the difference between a wise man and a smart man is that a smart man has learned through the mistakes of his past; however, a wise man is one who hires a smart man so he doesn't have to make the same mistakes that the smart man did. As a dreamer you have to be intentional in the way you build relationships around your dream. Your dream map can be realized at an exponential speed through association or geometric speed through your experience. The speed of actualizing your dream depends upon successful mentorship in your life. Find mentors with specialized knowledge within the locus of your dream. Who among your circle of influence has achieved you or is moving in the direction you want to go? "Where no counsel is, the people fall: but in the multitude of counselors there is safety."[3] Rally the right people around your dream. Building the right association around your dream increases your ability to achieve your dream. In the business world your net worth is proportionate to your network, so having the right people rallies the right resources to attain your dream.

> Your dream map can be realized at an exponential speed through association or geometric speed through your experience.

Your Dream Requires Teamwork

Every dreamer requires a group of people. Those whom you rally around you determine how far, how high, and how much of your dream you attain. You need people who can see what you are not seeing and

THE PRINCIPLE OF ASSOCIATIONS

have gone where you want to go. You need people who improve you, protect your focus, and empower your dream. You need people who are willing to work with you to achieve your goals.

> **Your dream needs to be so big that it takes others to dream with you.**

Inventory your associations, because relationships determine the resources you attract in your life. Don't misunderstand me as saying that people are to be used for selfish gain. Rather, God gives us relationships to help us pursue and complete our God-given mandate. The resources you need to achieve your dreams are tied into the relationships of your dream team. Most people who start the pursuit of their dreams have not yet mastered the expertise needed to fully accomplish their dreams. Though they are moving in the right direction, they are still unaware of some of their incompetence. Positive relationships will help you with this lack.

> *To be conscious that you are ignorant of the facts is a great step to knowledge.*
> Benjamin Disraeli

Surrounding yourself with people who are smarter than you not only brings awareness of your incompetence, but it enables you to learn from others. Nobody achieves a big dream alone; we must include others on our journey to realizing our dreams. Your dream needs to be so big that it takes others to dream with you. You can only be as powerful as the team you build, so assemble a winning team, and remember that teamwork makes the dream work. Your dream will require a variety of relationships. It makes a difference when you collaborate with visionaries and dreamers—people who purpose to make a difference. Connect with people who understand your dream and are motivated by your passion. "Iron sharpens iron, so a man sharpens the countenance of his friend."[4]

> **Your interaction with greatness will always birth intrinsic greatness in you.**

It requires energy to pursue your dreams, so surround yourself with people who inspire you, people who channel positive energy into your dream. Your interaction with greatness will always birth intrinsic greatness in you.

DREAM AXIOMS

- Associate with people who add value to your life and avoid those who discourage and stifle your dreams.

- Finding the right people to include in your life begins by evicting the wrong ones.

- You will get farther in life by avoiding people who are critical of your dreams

- We spend so much energy trying to please and prove our dreams to critics that we lose the energy needed to pursue our dreams.

- You become part of what or whom you are around.

- Life is full of people of mediocrity and those of excellence; choose whose influence you permit.

- Dreamers are fascinated with becoming exceptional; they are not content with mediocrity.

- Your dream map can be realized at an exponential speed through association or geometric speed through your experience.

- The speed of actualizing your dream depends upon successful mentorship in your life.

From Dreaming to Becoming

- Every dreamer requires a group of people. Those whom you rally around you determine how far, how high, and how much of your dream you attain.

- Your interaction with greatness will always birth intrinsic greatness in you.

Chapter 4

THE PRINCIPLE OF OWNERSHIP

The poorest man in the world is the man without a dream. The most frustrated man in the world is the man with a dream that never becomes a reality.

Dr. Myles Munroe

It is realistic to talk about having a dream when you have the means to pursue and accomplish your dream. But what if you are a child born into poverty, with no rich uncle or relatives to give you a hand up? Do you have the right to dream, and how realistic would your dream be? Would your dream be a possibility, or should dreaming be left to the select few who have connections and the infrastructure to make their dreams a reality? What if you were born premature with multiple physical illnesses and spent your childhood fighting for your life, going countless times to the emergency room of public hospitals yet receiving no specialized treatment because you had no insurance and could not afford a private doctor? What if all your days were devoid of even a splinter of hope, but filled with uncertainty if you would be alive one more day? Would you still candidate to dream? These are some of the questions I asked myself growing up in circumstances that allowed no room for hope that tomorrow would be any different from today.

You are probably wondering who Phinehas Kinuthia is and what gives me the authority to write about dreams. My above "what ifs" is my own story. I was born in Kenya, Africa, two months premature and weighed less than three pounds. My mother had a very complicated pregnancy. The doctors had advised she abort me, warning that if she didn't, she could be signing her own death certificate. Being a woman of faith and prayer, she chose life for me, even at the risk of losing hers. In preparation to sacrifice her life for her baby, my mom instructed my dad to take care of my elder sister and me. In recounting this experience, my heart grieves and tears blur my vision, knowing that it would have been easier for her to terminate the pregnancy and save her life. I was presumed to be a stillborn, but through my mother's faith and with the help of the doctors, I began to show vital signs. So began my difficult life.

Due to the lack of infrastructure and advanced medical facilities at the time, I developed chronic bronchitis and asthma and spent most of my childhood in and out of hospitals. I was physically feeble and so fragile that my mother would only wrap a blanket around me because she feared dressing me would break my bones. I was constantly on medication, which meant that I could not have a normal life like other children. While other children played outside, I watched from the sideline, avoiding any physical activity that would bring on severe asthma attacks. This significantly affected my self-esteem and how I viewed myself. I inwardly felt that I was not a normal child. I was obese and not athletic, so most children picked on me. It was not easy growing up with the stigma of being a premature-born, unhealthy, and inactive boy who stayed close to his mom all the time for fear of getting sick.

Several times I battled with other illnesses due to a weak immune system. I recall an incident at twelve years of age, when I was sick with malaria, typhoid, and had an asthma attack all at the same time. The doctors were unable to give a proper diagnosis and gave me an injection that numbed the entire left side of my body. We were so broke and could not afford a cab or to pay for a ride home that my mom had to carry me on her back, since I could not walk. In short, I had a traumatizing childhood.

Humble Beginnings

Some people are born into wealth and have several advantages, but that is not who I am. I was born into poverty. My parents were lower-class blue collar workers. My dad was a cab driver and made minimum wage working sixteen to eighteen hours a day, whereas my mother was a special education elementary school teacher for the deaf. We lived on $2 or less per day. We could not afford a balanced diet; chicken was a exceptional meal for Christmas and special occasions. We did not have the luxury of buying new clothes or shoes; we each had one set of "wash and wear" clothes—we washed them and waited for the clothes to dry before we wore them again. We wore the clothes until they were worn out, sometimes patching the holes to make them last longer.

Water is a basic necessity, but due to a high demand and low supply, the city would ration the water, so sometimes we had no water at all. We had to fetch water almost every week, and because water was scarce, we children would not shower every day. As a matter of fact, I did not know about underarm deodorant until I was twenty years old. We lived in a dilapidated house that bordered the slums. We related more with the poor, because we were always a month away from being homeless. Countless times we lost some of our personal belongings to the landlord in lieu of being evicted. My sister, brother, and I all shared one bedroom for years, until we grew up and moved out. Public schools in Kenya were not free at the time, but my parents struggled to put us all the way through high school. On several occasions we had to stay at home during the school year, since we did not have the tuition fees. Once I completed my high school education, my parents wanted me to further my education in college, but they were unable to pay the tuition. I searched for college opportunities and sponsorship to study in the Diaspora. When an opportunity finally opened for me to further my studies in the United States of America, my parents sold a small piece of land and held a fund-raiser, providing me with a one-way air ticket and $500. Registration for the school took $300, leaving me with $200 for books and bare necessities. The irony is that I was to attend a university that cost $12,000 per semester. My parents believed that sending me to such school in America, a land of opportunity, would allow me to work so that I could pay my tuition, cover my personal needs, and hopefully send money to help educate my other siblings. In other words, they were looking to me to be successful.

From Dreaming to Becoming

This was a very difficult time for me. I was a naïve boy who'd never had any exposure outside of his village, much less flown to a foreign land. I had no relatives or friends to help me acclimate to my new home in the United States. I was alone in a foreign land, with nothing more than a vague dream for a better future. Things got so hard that I began to lose hope for my dreams and started living a meaningless life and sometimes having suicidal thoughts.

> **Regardless of your past, you deserve to dream, so don't let others' standards of success limit your dream potential.**

It has been my experience and observation that society disregards people with my background and disqualifies them from being candidates of dreaming. When you grow up in poverty, your basic need is survival, to make it from day to day. Should you dare to dream, your background sets you at a disadvantage, and the odds are stacked against you to succeed. Today society in general judges success according to accomplishments, academic backgrounds, careers, income, and ancestry. But to measure success only on these parameters or in terms of material possessions disregards what is truly more valuable: personal satisfaction and fulfillment that comes from realized dreams.

I might not have a long list of accolades, but I am a witness that dreams do come true. Regardless of your past, you deserve to dream, so don't let others' standards of success limit your dream potential.

What's Your Story?

Some people have faced more dire situations than mine. My friend whose father shot his mother during the genocide in Rwanda was forced to watch horrific atrocities being committed against his family. Others are orphaned due to war; some were conceived as a result of rape, who loathe their existence and feel like they do not deserve to be alive. There are those who are born with disabilities, while others see their race as a debilitating thing and always blame their past for their present. While your past may be painful, your present has provided you with an opportunity to alter your future and bring you to a place of success. American author and poet Henry David Thoreau said, "I have learned this at least by my experiment: that if one advances confidently in the direction of his dreams, and endeavors to live the life which he has imagined, he will meet with a success unexpected in common hours."

We cannot negate that a disadvantaged start in your childhood may influence your success in life; however, complaining about and blaming your past or the government, re-electing a new president, marrying a new spouse, or getting a new job will not change your immediate current situation. Those who at some point in life have achieved anything of significant value had to take personal responsibility and ownership. In the words of Winston Churchill, "The price of greatness is responsibility." You cannot blame your parents, your employer, your education, your genetic disposition, or even the ebb and flow of life for how your life has turned out. Take responsibility for your actions to bring about change in your life. Don't let your past disappointments rob you of your dreaming opportunity today. Your future will be a result of your actions today. Start today to conceive and believe in your dream. Move toward your dream; pursue and become what you envision in your dreams.

> **Don't let your past disappointments rob you of your dreaming opportunity today. Your future will be a result of your actions today.**

The truth is we are daily either advancing toward our dreams or moving away from them. Refuse to be contained, and start moving toward your dream. Don't just envision your dream; make an effort to seize it.

The Price

The first step in becoming and achieving your dream is to own it, no matter how insignificant or disadvantaged you feel. Like many people, I complained and blamed God for my childhood. But change did not occur until I purposed in my heart to embrace and pursue my own dreams. Challenges will always be a part of life, and you cannot put off dreaming until you eliminate your undesirable conditions or change your unwanted position in life. You have to grab your dream by the horns, because your dream is your ticket out of a life of misery. Your dream is like a seed planted in your heart that takes time to grow and mature before it can produce fruit. And it doesn't happen by accident. You have to cultivate that seed if you intend to reap the fruits of your dream. It wasn't until I began to pursue my dream that life started having meaning and excitement.

We read about Joseph in the Bible who had a dream. His dream birthed in him a passion to pursue his future. He began to share his dream with so much excitement and enthusiasm that people associate him with his dream. When his brothers saw him, they identified him by saying, "Behold this dreamer is coming."[1] In his book *Put your Dream to a Test*, John Maxwell posits, "If you want to accomplish a dream you will be able to do so only when you can see it clearly. You must

From Dreaming to Becoming

define it before you can pursue it. Most people don't do that. Their dream remains a dream—something fuzzy and unspecific. As a result they never achieve it."[2] To move from dreaming to becoming, your dream has to be clear and must be your personal obsession. Your dream is not merely a passing thought; your dream stays with you. When the right dream finds the right person, an inseparable force is created. Your dream seed implants within you.

Own your dream

Do you have a conviction concerning your dream? Are you willing to work on your dream day or night, to pursue your dream at all cost? Is it worth sacrificing your sleep, risking your comfort, and investing all your resource before you see any returns? Are you prepared to overcome obstacles and fight through adversity and rejection to fulfill your dream? If you answered yes to these questions, then you are beginning to own your dream.

> *This is the soulful meaning of happiness:*
> *to live the life that is truly ours, to give*
> *the most of who we essentially are.*
>
> Jack Weber

The Principle of Ownership

International author, speaker, and expert on wisdom, Dr. Mike Murdock states, "The proof of desire is pursuit."[3] Whenever you are passionate about your dream, you will pursue your dream at all cost. Dr. Martin Luther King Jr. strongly believed that "A man who won't die for something is not fit to live." Thomas Edison is said to have claimed that many people thought he was smart, but on the contrary, while most people think of many things daily, he would think of only one thing daily. He had more respect for a person who accomplished a single idea than one who had a thousand ideas and did nothing.

> **I would rather have one dream that defines me than many dreams that remain undefined.**

I would rather have one dream that defines me than many dreams that remain undefined. Realize that your dream cannot be merely a passing thought or wishful thinking but a dominant idea that governs your life's pursuits. As a dreamer it is your responsibility to protect and defend the mental image of your dream. Do not lose sight of the main thing, which is your dream. Narrow your focus to your dream. Too often we waste time pursuing everything but our dreams.

You will never attain your dream without unwavering passion. Cary Fiorina, former chairman and CEO of Hewlett-Packard, advised, "Love what you do, or don't do it. Don't make a choice of any kind, whether in career or in life, just because it pleases others or because it ranks high on someone else's scale of achievement. Make the choice to do something because it engages your heart as well as your mind. Make a choice because it engages all of you."[4] Steve Jobs echoed this very thought in a speech he gave at the Stanford commencement ceremony in 2005: "You have to find what you truly love. The only way to be truly satisfied is to do what you believe is a great work and the only way to do a great work is to love what you do. If you haven't found it yet, keep looking. Don't settle."[5]

Most people who move from dreaming to becoming have honed their energy and effort to a specific dream. The reason we identify with athletes like Michael Jordan, Barry Bonds, Serena Williams, and Tiger Woods is because over the years they have focused on their gifts and relentlessly pursued their dreams to be arguably the best in their disciplines. In the words of Zig Ziglar, "They are no longer wandering generalities but have become meaningful specifics." The apostle Paul, writing to the Philippians said, "I do not count myself to have apprehended; but one thing I do, forgetting those things which are behind and reaching forward to those things which are ahead."[6] Your dream needs to be the one thing that defines you. Your dream must dominate you. Can others identify you with your dream?

Is it your dream, or are you living on borrowed dreams? If you never own your dreams, you will never have the confidence to attain them. In his book the *Traveler's Gift*, Andy Andrews wrote, "As I sleep, the same dream that dominates my waking hours will be with me in the dark. Yes, I have a dream. It is a great dream, and I will never apologize for it. Neither will I ever let it go, for if I did, my life will be finished. My hopes, my passions for my vision for the future are my very existence. A person without a dream never had a dream come true."[7]

> *Dream no small dreams for they have no power to move the hearts of men.*
> Johann Wolfgang von Goethe

The True Value of Your Dream

What dream is in your heart? Is your dream only about you? How does your dream potentially influence your life and the life of others around you? While you should own your dream, I believe that almost always a great dream should not be about us but should be about the welfare of others. Albert Einstein said, "Only a life lived for others is a life worthwhile." Most people tend to see a dream as a key to attaining possessions, wealth, power, fame, luxury, or prestige—maybe largely because of what the "American Dream" is portrayed to be.

> **Your dream has to be value driven and not only possessions motivated.**

Your dream has to be value driven and not only possessions motivated. A great dream will equip others to experience a better way of life. For example, Dr. Martin Luther King Jr., and Mother Teresa had dreams that outlive their lifespans and transcend their personal interests. Inventory the authenticity of your dream to determine its fulfillment potential. A dream that is lived for only one's personal satisfaction or fulfillment is nothing more than a personal ambition. Your dream is greater than who you are or what you will ever be in your lifetime. A true dream will outlive the dreamer. A few months ago, America dedicated a memorial to Dr. Martin Luther King Jr., almost forty-three years after his death, and his dream continues to flourish. True dreams have longevity beyond the dreamer.

> Have you tested your dream through the lens of your beliefs?

What do you believe of your dream?

Are you inspired to think or see yourself living in your dream?

Believe in Your Dream

What you believe in determines how far and high you reach. God will work with what we believe within the confines of His purpose in our lives. We do so little because we have lost belief and expectation that our dreams will ever become a reality. You cannot give up on your dream, for when you do, you lose the courage to face tomorrow's uncertainties. Believing in your dream is not passive; believing requires that we be on the lookout with great expectation, talking and acting like it must happen at anytime. You don't get what you deserve in life; rather, you get what you believe in and act on. This was echoed in Jesus's statement, "Believe that you will receive them and you shall have them."[8]

> **Rationalizing failure approves failure in your life. So stop making excuses for failure and overcome it.**

Most people have little or no expectancy concerning their future. Whenever we are faced with multiple challenges and hardships, we have a proclivity to adopt a philosophy that accommodates our present situations. We tend to justify and rationalize our condition instead of provoking ourselves to change our circumstances. Rationalizing failure approves failure in your life. So stop making excuses for failure and overcome it.

> **While every dream has the potential of reward, the reward is the product of the dream and not the dream itself.**

Success in attaining your dream is not equated to the amount of wealth you accumulate. You could be wealthy but dissatisfied. Though the world measures success in terms of material possessions, we could go deeper and say that ultimate success is more of who you become and what you accomplish relative to who you were intended to be. Some belief systems propagate the wrong ideas and thoughts, which have influenced our beliefs and made us equate attaining our dreams to accumulation of wealth or the lack of it thereof. While every dream has the potential of reward, the reward is the product of the dream and not the dream itself. I have seen the frustration and disappointment such belief systems bring to those living in poverty, which tends toward despair and pessimism. Growing up in Kenya, the prevailing thought of the poor in response to the wealthy was that the wealthy must have been involved in occultism or satanic worship to have acquired such wealth. Similarly in the United States, the poor have adopted a philosophy that those who are wealthy are unhappy and have obtained their success through unjust enrichment. These are self-reaffirming and misguided ideas that some people adopt as opiates to pacify their own poverty consciousness. Whereas on the other hand, the wealthy tend to look down on the poor, believing that a lower level of living is the poor's natural predisposition and a result of their hereditary, environment, or lack of a conscious effort on their part to change their situation. Truth be told, you can live your dream without accumulation of wealth. Mother Teresa lived her dream and was not on Forbes list of the world's wealthiest people. Discard these limiting beliefs that create the illusion that unless you have wealth or material, you are not living or fulfilling your dream.

Too many people see their dreams as a myth or a utopian ideal that is so farfetched it is never attainable. Our dreams are often to us like a young minority child or a female child who grew up saying that one day she would become the president of the United States. While the parents would probably go along with their child's belief, in their hearts they knew the limitations of such a dream and deep down would not think much of such a dream because it was farfetched. Some parents would never perceive or fathom the reality of such a child's dream. But soon after the first minority president, Barack Obama, was elected, suddenly their belief system was altered.

Never Limit Your Dreams

For a young man from Kenya, born into nothing, within the slopes of inadequacy and living among the disenfranchised, I had a tendency to limit myself to the circumstances of my life and my environment. My dream was limited to what seemed attainable from my present resources. I never thought beyond having enough to meet my daily need. The thought of impacting the world was incomprehensible. It was not until I changed my belief system that my life started changing. I had to come to terms with myself and take inventory of my beliefs. I had to embrace the understanding that there is more out there for me than I presently experienced.

> Regardless of where you are now, your dream is not a fantasy; it can become a reality.

There is nothing wrong with being born in the ghetto; some successful people have come from there. Just don't let the ghetto mind-set dictate or limit your dreams. Regardless of where you are now, your dream is not a fantasy; it can become a reality. You can achieve your dream, but you need to change your belief system. Do not confine your dreams to the circumference of your circumstance, learn to dream big.

Maryanne Wilson attributed the following to President Nelson Mandela's inaugural speech in 1994: "Our deepest fear is not that we are inadequate. Our deepest fear is that we are powerful beyond measure." You are only powerful beyond measure when you locate yourself at the center of God's will for your life. When you find your purpose, you locate your potential. Own your dream. Don't shrink to fit into the mediocrity that exists around you. We know this to be true because Henry David Thoreau affirms that "the masses of men lead lives of quiet desperation."

Do not blame situations and other people for where you are; start seeing yourself living in your dream. The best way to own your dream is to evaluate the authenticity of your dream. Put your dream through a test. A dream that is never tested will most likely never be realized. Once your dream is tested, it becomes clear. Until your dream becomes clear, it's only an idea. In his book *Dare to Dream*, author John Maxwell posits these questions that everyone should ask about their dream:

> Does your dream inspire you to work hard?
> Does your dream motivate you to take smart risks?

From Dreaming to Becoming

Does your dream build you up?
Will your dream benefit others around you?
As you move closer to fulfilling your dream, will your dream bring you closer to who you were born to be?[9]

DREAM AXIOMS

- Regardless of your past, you deserve to dream, so don't let others' standards of success limit your dream potential.

- Don't let your past disappointments rob you of your dreaming opportunity today.

- Your future will be a result of your actions today.

- We are daily either advancing toward our dreams or moving away from them.

- Realize that your dream cannot be merely a passing thought or wishful thinking but a dominant idea that governs your life's pursuits.

- To move from dreaming to becoming, your dream has to be clear and must be your personal obsession.

- Have one dream that defines you rather than many dreams that remain undefined.

- It is your responsibility to protect and defend the mental image of your dream.

- Your dream needs to be the one thing that defines you. Your dream must dominate you.

From Dreaming to Becoming

- Your dream has to be value driven and not possessions motivated.

- A dream that is lived for only one's personal satisfaction or fulfillment is nothing more than a personal ambition.

- A true dream will outlive the dreamer.

- Your dream is greater than who you are or what you will ever be in your lifetime.

- God will work with what we believe within the confines of His purpose in our lives.

- Rationalizing failure approves failure in your life. Stop making excuses for failure and overcome it.

- Regardless of where you are now, your dream is not a fantasy; it can become a reality.

- Do not confine your dreams to the circumference of your circumstance, learn to dream big.

- Narrow your focus to your dream.

- A dream that is never tested will most likely never be realized.

Chapter 5

THE PRINCIPLE OF PREPARATION

Before anything else, getting ready is the secret of success.

Henry Ford

True dreamers who move from dreaming to becoming are cognizant of their need for preparation. They dress up for where they are going, not where they have been. Most people never attempt to prepare for where they want to be in life. We are so fixated on where we have been and the struggles we have encountered that we fail to see what lies ahead. To move from dreaming to becoming, we have to let go of things that happened in our past and start preparation for that which we seek in our near future. If you are not careful, your past will camouflage your future, making it seem insignificant. Dr. Myles Munroe, in his book *Releasing Your Potential*, wrote, "We may not be able to change our past, and our future might be unlived, but the present provides us with the opportunity to maximize our ability."[1] Those who move from dreaming to becoming are careful to extract the potential from their present, because they anticipate their future to be wrapped in their present.

> **Those who move from dreaming to becoming are careful to extract the potential from their present, because they anticipate their future to be wrapped in their present.**

Benjamin Disraeli asserted, "The secret of life is for man to be ready for his time when it comes." Preparation precedes opportunity; opportunity will favor only the prepared. You must become your own opportunity. Life was not meant to be a walk in the park, for life is full of challenges, and only those who are prepared will rise to its challenges and become uncommon achievers. King Solomon in his wisdom wrote, "I returned, and saw under the sun, that the race is not to the swift, nor the battle to the strong, neither yet bread to the wise, nor yet riches to men of understanding, nor yet favor to men of skill; but time and chance happened to them all."[2]

Preparation is never time wasted but time invested. Most people are never ready when the opportunities arise because they never invested time in preparation. Those who did prepare are ready to take advantage of opportunities the moment they arrive. Start making preparation for your dream, even if it means doing a little at a time, starting from where you are today. Joseph started practicing to interpret dreams while he was yet in prison. If Pharaoh did not have a dream, if Joseph had not prepared himself, he would have rotted in prison. God has given someone a dream that He is preparing you to solve, and your promotion is tied to your ability to be ready when that moment comes.

Are You Planning to Fail?

It's a common saying that failing to plan is planning to fail. How do you execute a big plan? When I studied project management, the prevailing thought was that we must first establish a plan and then implement the plan to accomplish the project. It is in planning that goals or desired outcomes become clear. Without a plan it's impossible to measure progress. One has to compare actual progress with planned progress to determine any levels of success and establish any necessary corrective action. So if you have no plan, how would you know that you are making progress toward your dream? A dream without a plan is a delusion.

From Dreaming to Becoming

William Jennings Bryant said, "Destiny is not a matter of choice. It is not something to be waited for but rather something to be achieved." I believe that destiny is not unpredictable. Destiny is scheduled by your present actions. Dreams don't just happen; dreams are first clarified, pursued, and then achieved. God's will for your life is not automatic, but it requires your participation.

A dream without a plan is a delusion.

I have learned to be actively participating with God in making my dream a reality. Sometimes God answers our prayers through the plans He gives us in form of ideas. It is the initiation of these ideas that births our advancement toward our dreams. The Bible says, "A man's heart plans his way, But the Lord directs his steps."[3] Planning is necessary before any undertakings. God gave David a detailed plan for the building of the temple, and He provided Noah with the blueprint for the ark. In His teachings Jesus talked about the importance of preparation: "For which of you, intending to build a tower, does not sit down first and count the cost, whether he has enough to finish it lest, after he has laid the foundation, and is not able to finish all who see it begin to mock him, saying, 'This

The Principle of Preparation

man began to build and was not able to finish'? Or what king, going to make war against another king, does not sit down first and consider whether he is able with ten thousand to meet him who comes against him or with twenty thousand."[4] Your dream is no exception; it requires a plan of execution.

> **Dreams don't just happen; dreams are first clarified, pursued, and then achieved.**

David Schwartz, author of *The Magic of Thinking Big*, wrote, "A goal is more than a dream; it's a dream being acted upon."[5] Preparation starts with goal setting; however, you must ensure that your goals are congruent with your assignment. When you define your goals, you refine your faith and get clarity for what you are pursuing. Once you define a goal, the steps necessary to obtain it come into view. Having goals bring dreams to life. You cannot attain and become anything that you have not set goals for. Setting goals increases your ability to produce and accomplish more. Goals propel us toward our desired plan. Motivation expert Les Brown said, "Goals help you channel your energy into action." Orrin Woodward added to that thought, "Goals are a planned assault on the status quo."

Goal Setting

Most people don't plan but rather *wish* that one day they will be successful. A wish is a dream without a goal. Perhaps we fail to plan for fear of a negative outcome in case we fail to meet our target, or maybe we are just intimidated by the process because of the demands of following through to accomplish the goals we set. Some are unfamiliar with the process because no one ever taught them how to set goals. Whatever your case might be, goals are necessary in developing an action plan.

> Destiny is not unpredictable.
> Destiny is scheduled by your
> present actions.

Writing out your goals eliminates obscurity from your plan of action. I must emphasize that having *and* writing your goals is an imperative necessity in achieving your dreams. People with goals are always accomplishing more than people without them. It is said that 3 percent of adults have clearly written goals and the remaining 97 percent of people work for them. Goals are a plan of action for pursuing and attaining your dreams. Dreams become realities only when pursued. According to Jim Rohn, America's leading business authority on success, "If you go to work on your goals, your goals will go to work on you. If you go to work on your plan, your plan will go to work on you. Whatever good things we build end up building us." This is why we must invest our resources in executing a great plan for the pursuit of our goals. In goal setting we nurture our dreams, and the dreams we nurture are the people we become.

> The more reasons you have for attaining your dream, the more motivation you will have for pursuing it.

In his *Success Mastery System*, which I strongly recommend, Brian Tracy, arguably America's best coach on goal setting, claims that his proven systematic process or blueprint for goal setting will increase your likelihood of achieving goals by about 1000 percent, or ten times greater than not using the process.

Write it Down

The first step is to write down your dreams and visualize what your dream will look like. How strongly do you desire your dream? Establish how important your dream is and write it down to make it plain. Lee Iacocca stated it this way: "The discipline of writing something down is the first step towards making it happen." Writing down your dream demystifies it and gives you possibilities for attaining it. The more reasons you have for attaining your dream, the more motivation you will have for pursuing it. Begin with where you are; be honest with yourself about where you are in life. A well-known Chinese proverb says, "A journey of 1000 miles starts with a single step." You have to begin somewhere.

> **Your dreams will always be diminished to the same level as your inability to set, pursue, and achieve definite goals.**

An indefinite goal will always produce indefinite results. Your dreams will always be diminished to the same level as your inability to set, pursue, and achieve definite goals. Apart from setting specific goals that are smart, measurable, attainable, and realistic, your goals must be timely. Those who move from dreaming to becoming understand timing is vital to their dreams. There is a time for everything under the earth. You don't have eternity on earth, so learning to make your time count is necessary in achieving your goals. Tasks will always expand or diminish proportionate to the time you designate to them. In order to achieve goals, we must not only set a deadline but also set sub-deadlines on each intermediate goal. Concrete dreams have deadlines.

Set Deadlines

A goal is a dream with a deadline; therefore, when you set a dream, break it into small, achievable increments. Breaking big dreams into smaller, manageable parts makes the dream more attainable, creates a sense of short-term fulfillment, and builds motivation. If you have a dream of completing your PhD, start with deadlines for your high school diploma or your GED. Another deadline would be for your associate diploma, then your undergraduate diploma, followed by your postgraduate, and so on. A deadline is a forcing system, and the more deadlines you have, the more chances you have to achieve the dream. People dream of being millionaires and yet they have not attained the smaller goal of reaching their first $100,000, which makes their dream unrealistic and unattainable. You must break down your goal into small increments. Success is in attaining small, progressive goals toward a larger worthwhile goal. People don't just become lucky in life. You determine your own luck by your actions, actions that move you daily toward your goals.

The secret of your future is hidden in your daily routine.

Dr. Mike Murdock

Identify Obstacles

Once you have set your deadlines, identify and inventory the obstacles you will need to overcome. Obstacles are meant to bring out the best in you; they unlock potential you never knew existed. To the unprepared, an obstacle is a crisis, but to those who expect obstacles, they become a catalyst for advancement and an opportunity providing direction toward greatness. A dreamer is not intimidated by crisis but is inspired by it. When obstacles show up in our path toward our goals, they indicate a correction is necessary, but only a change in direction and not the change of goals. Obstacles are detour signs to your goals and not end-of-the-road signs. When we encounter detours on a construction site, we follow the signs that direct us to an alternate route that will lead us to our original destination, which didn't change.

> **To the unprepared, an obstacle is a crisis, but to those who expect obstacles, they become a catalyst for advancement and an opportunity providing direction toward greatness**

Sometimes we put obstacles in our path. What obstacles have you consciously or subconsciously erected that stand between you and the attainment of your destiny? Is it procrastination, fear, lack of skills, self-constraints, or age? Whatever it is, don't let it stop you. There will always be an obstacle that stands between you and your goal. Where great goals can be attained, great obstacles exist. Your greatest obstacle will be your greatest opportunity; therefore, do not give up. Dreamers reach for their dreams and they are not deterred by obstacles. Find a way to overcome or go around obstacles. There are no limitations that are exceptional, only those we accept.

This brings me to the point emphasized in the book *Flip Side* by Flip Flippen. "Strengths alone do not single-handedly define our success. No matter how formidable our talents, we are held back by behaviors that set limits for our performance or define the reasons for our failure."[6] And these become obstacles to attaining our dreams. It is in identifying these constraints and overcoming them that we see a dramatic surge in success, productivity, and happiness in all aspects of our life. Therefore, if we are to live fully and achieve our goals, we can and should learn how to minimize behavioral weaknesses while maximizing our strengths.

In *Goal Setting*, Dr. Mike Murdock emphasizes that writing your vision creates a mental image. You can only do something you can see; you must see a goal before you can reach it because written goals matter more. Allow me to reiterate that failing to plan is planning to fail. You must make things happen for you instead of waiting for things just to happen. If we sit back and not take responsibility, we will fit into other people's plans rather than designing our own plans. Most people have dreams but never value their dreams enough to document them on paper and create timelines to bring their dreams to life.

Once you reach this stage of goal setting, the next step is to determine what you possess to morally and ethically achieve your goals. Develop the action plan, the path of least resistance, and the steps to take to advance toward your goals. Prioritize your plan according to the right sequence of events.

Ask yourself these questions to help you determine how prepared you are:

1. What successful events and failures in my past must I embrace and move on?
2. What will it mean to achieve my dreams, and how will it impact my life if I don't?
3. What action steps must I take to prepare for my dreams?
4. What goals have I set and am I willing to set concerning my dreams?
5. Do I have a deadline and sub-deadlines scheduled within the timetable of my goals?

6. Am I truly committed and prepared to succeed and achieve these goals?
7. What are the obstacles and the limitations I must overcome to achieve my goals?

DREAM AXIOMS

- True dreamers who move from dreaming to becoming are cognizant of their need for preparation. They dress up for where they are going, not where they have been.

- If you are not careful, your past will camouflage your future, making it seem insignificant.

- Preparation precedes opportunity; opportunity will favor only the prepared.

- Destiny is not unpredictable. Destiny is scheduled by your present actions.

- Dreams don't just happen; dreams are first clarified, pursued, and then achieved.

- God's will for your life is not automatic, but it requires your participation.

- When you define your goals, you refine your faith and get clarity for what you are pursuing.

- Writing out your goals eliminates obscurity from your plan of action.

- A dream without a plan is a delusion.

The Principle of Preparation

- Goals are a plan of action for pursuing and attaining your dreams.

- Your dreams will always be diminished to the same level as your inability to set, pursue, and achieve definite goals.

- To the unprepared, an obstacle is a crisis, but to those who expect obstacles, they become a catalyst for advancement an opportunity providing direction toward greatness.

- Obstacles are detour signs to your goals and not end-of-the-road signs.

- Your greatest obstacle will be at your greatest opportunity; do not give up.

- There are no limitations that are exceptional, only those we accept.

Chapter 6

THE PRINCIPLE OF PERSPIRATION

A dream doesn't become reality through magic; it takes sweat, determination and hard work.

Colin Powell

Indecision can cripple even the best dreamer. Most people are indecisive and will not take the first action step to pursue their dreams. In his book *177 Mental Toughness*, Steve Siebold underscores the importance of developing a sound decision-making process while understanding that every decision is somewhat a gamble, which is the foundation of champions. "Amateur performers habitually play not to lose and procrastinate because they fear making a mistake. The great ones know mistakes will be made and can be corrected."[1]

> **Good thinking needs to be transformed into good actions. Action transcends thoughts. Good thoughts without action are as detrimental as bad thoughts with action.**

Many dreamers fail to realize their dreams because they are waiting for the stars to align or until conditions are right. For fear of making a mistake, some wait to begin the pursuit of their dreams, while others wait for the perfect timing—that is when no obstacles exists. These folks are doomed to fail before they take a single step. If you wait for perfect conditions, you will never get anything done. Thomas Edison said, "Genius is one percent inspiration and ninety-nine percent perspiration." No matter how great and effective your dream is, you have to work it out. Your dream is transformed by action. Good thinking needs to be transformed into good actions. Action transcends thoughts. Good thoughts without action are as detrimental as bad thoughts with action.

> *A good plan violently executed now,*
> *is better than a perfect plan*
> *executed next week.*
>
> George Patton

There will never be a perfect time to implement your dream. Make a decision and be proactive. Stop making excuses and just do it. In the words of Andy Andrews, "Successful people make their decision quickly and change their minds slowly. Failures make their decisions slowly and change their minds quickly."[2] There are no magical moments for your dream; there are just moments, and when we seize these moments, we make them magical. Learn to develop and work on your dreams as you progress. A true dreamer is a person of action, one who moves forward toward the attainment of his or her dream. Your dream will become a reality only when you pursue it. Nothing will happen to a dream you do nothing about.

> **There are no magical moments for your dream; there are just moments, and when we seize these moments, we make them magical.**

Settle in your mind this fact: There will never be a time when your plan is flawless. God uses flawed vessels to attain his flawless plan. Even the best of plans have contingencies if Plan A does not go as presumed.

Those who move from dreaming to becoming are progressively pursuing their dreams. They understand that dreams take time and continuous course corrections

The Principle of Perspiration

before becoming realities. There is no such thing as overnight success, but what we perceive as overnight success has been a work in progress; it has been success in the making for days, months, years, and maybe decades.

> *Patience, persistence and perspiration*
> *make an unbeatable combination*
> *for success.*
> — Napoleon Hill

There will never be a time when your plan is flawless. God uses flawed vessels to attain His flawless plan.

Don't give up on first attempts because something you tried does not work. Keep going. You owe it to yourself and others who come after you to become everything you are intended to be. Your potential is revealed as you act on your dreams. What if Abraham Lincoln had given up when he had a nervous breakdown and was bedridden for six months? What if he had decided not to run for the presidency after running for congress and losing four times? What if he had given up on life after his fiancée died days before their wedding? I have come to terms with the truth that perfection is something I will continually pursue, even though it doesn't exist. Do not allow the lack of perfection or the presence of failure to stop you from pursuing your dreams. Start somewhere and start somehow. Begin to use what you have and quit worrying over what you lack.

> *The real tragedy of life is not in being limited to one talent but in the failure to use one talent.*
>
> Edgar W. Work

Responsibility

Those who move from dreaming to becoming are self-leaders; they lead by doing, they are decisive, and they lead themselves to pursue their dreams. Winston Churchill said that the price of greatness is responsibility. No one else will make your dream a reality but you, so who are you waiting for? Build your dreams instead of hoping that your dreams will somehow happen. Take initiative and responsibility for your dreams. In the words of Johann Wolfgang von Goethe, "Whatever you do, or dream you can, begin it. Boldness has quite some genius, power, and magic in it. Never reduce yourself to being just a career dreamer for it takes courage for one to afford to translate their dreams into a reality. Anybody can dream but it takes a pragmatist risk taker to live his or her dreams." If your dream is to become a published author, start writing and don't worry about which publishing company to pitch it to. If your dream is to compose Grammy Award–winning songs, start composing and do not concern yourself about who will produce it. We allow things that are not immediately necessary to stop us from taking the initial step. Do not allow what you cannot accomplish to influence what you are capable of completing.

> **Your dream will be realized in increments of progressions. It's a continuum of decisions, actions, and events, so start working on your dream.**

In the words of St. Francis of Assisi, "You start by doing what's necessary; then do what's possible; and suddenly you are doing the impossible." We set for ourselves self-limiting excuses, which become the nails that build our houses of failure. I believe that when the student is ready the teacher emerges. Cross the bridge when you get to that bridge, but until then keep doing what you know to do until you get to where you need help. Your dream will be realized in increments of progressions. It's a continuum of decisions, actions, and events, so start working on your dream. The pursuit of

From Dreaming to Becoming

your dream is not a momentous high that is satisfied temporarily and immediately, but it's a journey that one pursues perpetually until the dream is fully realized.

> **Your dream will always remain obscure until an external force created by your actions is applied to it.**

Newton's first law of motion states that every object persists in its state of rest or uniform motion in a straight line unless it is compelled to change that state by forces impressed on it. Your dream will always remain obscure until an external force created by your actions is applied to it. The quality of your goal doesn't necessarily guarantee the fulfillment of it; you must labor to make your dream a reality. John Maxwell rightfully stated, "Dreams don't work unless you do." Start working on your dream. Be courageous, seize every moment that your current opportunity has presented to you. The journey toward a big dream begins with a small start. In his book *Wooden: A Lifetime Observation and Reflection On and Off the Court*, author Coach John Wooden with Steve Jamison lends us some inspiration: "You have to apply yourself each day to become better. By applying yourself to the task of becoming a little better each day and every day, over a period of time you will become a lot better. Only then will you be able to approach being the best you can be. It begins by trying to make each day count and knowing that you can never make up for lost day."³

A humorous story will help your understanding. A minister nearing retirement purchased a small abandoned farm outside town. The house was in dire need of maintenance. The windows were broken. The paint peeled from the scorching summer sun. The roof leaked. The porch had a series of potholes. Weeds were plentiful. Debris and litter scattered the landscape. The fence was all but gone. On his weekly day off, the minister worked on the farm. He was diligent. He did a little here, a little there. In an amazingly short period of time, this once dilapidated farm became a showpiece. Friends and townspeople were impressed with the minister's work.

One day the minister's neighbor from town came to visit the country cottage. The awed city dweller gawked at the garden growing out back, the newly restored house and barn, and the beautiful landscaping. He said, "You and the Lord really did a marvelous work here."

The minister looked up from his workbench, where he was building garden benches. He wiped the perspiration from his eyes. He thought for a moment, and then replied, "Yea, but you should have seen it when the Lord had it all to himself."

This story is a reflection of the passive nature in us that waits on God to do everything. Most people say that God is in control, so they believe that if God meant for them to have something, then they would have it. God is certainly in control, but He has put you behind the wheel and given you the ability to do something through the decisions you make.

DREAM AXIOMS

- Indecision can cripple even the best dreamers.

- Your dream is transformed by action. Good thinking needs to be transformed into good actions.

- Good thoughts without action are as detrimental as bad thoughts with action.

- There are no magical moments for your dream; there are just moments, and when we seize these moments, we make them magical.

- Do not allow the lack of perfection or the presence of failure to stop you from pursuing your dreams.

- Never allow things that are not immediately necessary to stop you from taking the first step in pursuit of your dream.

- Nothing will happen to a dream you do nothing about. Your dream will become a reality only when you pursue it.

- God uses flawed vessels to attain His flawless plan.

- Those who move from dreaming to becoming are progressively pursuing their dreams.

From Dreaming to Becoming

- Your dream will be realized in increments of progressions. It's a continuum of decisions, actions, and events, so start working on your dream.

- The pursuit of your dream is not a momentous high that is satisfied temporarily and immediately, but it's a journey that one pursues perpetually until the dream is fully realized.

- Your dream will always remain obscure until an external force created by your actions is applied to it.

Chapter 7

THE PRINCIPLE OF TRADEOFFS

For everything you have missed, you have gained something else; and for everything you gain, you lose something.
         Ralph Waldo Emerson

Beverly Sills, a great opera star, has said that there are no shortcuts to any place worth going. Most people have dreams but do not want to pay the price to become what they want. We want to have our cake and eat it too. The truth is that those who move from dreaming to becoming have chosen to pay the price and have made significant sacrifices. There is a price for every progress. Great heights demand of us great sacrifices. We first have to do what we don't want to do, so we can enjoy second what we want. A true dreamer has to make some trade-offs or some equitable exchanges to make his or her dream a reality. Trade-offs will be required at different levels of your growth journey. The trade-offs you make in your twenties might not be the same as you would make at age fifty, but trade-offs are an inevitable part of life; therefore, it's imperative to make the right tradeoffs to accomplish your dreams. Tradeoff is the price you pay to maintain focus on the journey from dreaming to becoming. Without trade-offs, you will never attain your full potential, and your dream will be downgraded to a lower level of achievement. In his INJOY Life Club, John Maxwell discusses some of the necessary trade-offs: "You must give up to go up." (This is also referred to as the Law of Sacrifice in John's *21 Irrefutable Laws of Leadership*.)

> **Trade-off is the price you pay to maintain focus on the journey from dreaming to becoming.**

The following trade-offs are not necessarily in order of priority or importance, but they are necessary. I have learned over the years that uncommon achievers and successful people practice these trade-offs.

1. Trade Off People's Affirmation for Personal Accomplishments

Trading affirmation for accomplishment has greatly impacted my life. Those who move from dreaming to becoming have to trade off affirmation for accomplishment. I grew up in a family in which decisions were not celebrated, I had no role models, and no one cheered me up when I was sad. As a result, I became fond of my peers' approval. You may have experienced a similar situation. Your performance earns you the trophies and name recognition. Applause secures a seat for you at your peers' table. The praise and approval makes you believe that you are making progress in the right direction. The cheerleaders in your life become the yardsticks of success and progress. But as you move into maturity, you understand that people celebrate you when it's convenient for them and as long as it doesn't challenge their status quo.

Don't be pigeonholed to sit at the seat of mediocrity because you want to relate to people in your past. Mediocrity, after a while, will always reward mediocrity. Be careful of people in your past who don't add value but linger to push guilt into your life. They are constantly claiming how much you have changed and that you are not who you used to be simply because they can't understand, confine, and control you anymore.

These kinds of people are detrimental to your progress. The truth is you are changing; like living organisms, you were created for growth.

> **Don't seek endorsement from people who have not sailed the seas you are pioneering.**

Most people who seek approval from others in everything they do never realize their dreams. Whenever you declare your dream, you proclaim a season of adversity, so expect and welcome opposition. The mistake we make is that we seek affirmation from people who don't want to see us succeed. Your dream will always provoke anger in non-dreamers. We wait on their approval to step into our dreams. Don't seek endorsement from people who have not sailed the seas you are pioneering. You must decide between affirmation from your peers or accomplishing your God-given dream. Start moving and begin to accomplish bigger things in life.

2. Trade Off Instant Gratification for Future Fulfillment

Dreamers are willing to forsake present gratification to pursue their dreams for the joy of future fulfillment. We live in a society that wants everything now. We are

The Principle of Tradeoffs

accustomed to the instant world, instant downloads, drive-through fast-food joints, and companies that promote push-button results. Marketing firms are making money from products that promise quick results. Companies adopt slogans that promise quick, painless, effortless results at the push of a button or the swallow of a pill. "Lose 50 pounds in one week! No exercising and no gimmicks!" Credit card companies make credit instantly accessible to the unqualified, who then can experience instant gratification at the expense of their future. We have mortgaged our future and degraded the quality of our lives, and as a result we live unfulfilled; always paying debts and being a slave to the lender. We want reward without work, performance without preparation, and action without a plan.

As I previously said, your dream will be realized in increments of progressions; it's a continuum of decisions, actions, and events. Your dream will be realized over a long period of time. Your dream is progressive. The lottery mentality of somehow realizing a dream one day when everything falls perfectly into place or enjoying a return without having made an investment will not work. Invest your time and resources to attain your most desired dream. Cultivate your dream; get information and research about becoming the best in what you desire. You will invest quality time only in that which you value or love. This process is an ongoing

From Dreaming to Becoming

result of self-discipline and perseverance. I have learned that to attain my dreams, I have to deny myself that which I want to enjoy now in exchange for what I want to become tomorrow. Make the necessary sacrifices now and choose to go without. Make exceptions to channel all your resources to your dream first, then your dream will provide the resources for your ambitions.

> **Make exceptions to channel all your resources to your dream first, then your dream will provide the resources for your ambitions.**

3. Trade Off Immediate Pleasure for Personal Growth

Most people want greatness, but they do not want to pay the price tag for it. I learned a long time ago that to become indispensable, I had to become more valuable through personal growth. Some people ask, How do you earn more in the marketplace? The answer is to become more valuable. For instance, the education and training that a lawyer or a surgeon attains makes them more valuable than a custodian. I say this not to be flippant, because both precious human beings are created by the same God and He values them equally; however, the surgeon or the attorney through personal growth maximized the opportunity afforded them, which makes them more valuable *in the marketplace* because of the problems they solve. Sir William James, a British Naval commander during World War 1, said, "The problems we face cannot be solved at the level of thinking in which they were created." You must give up the good things that you want to enjoy now, for what you want to become later. Growth brings good things; good things don't bring growth. I believe that internal growth brings about external growth; as within so without.

> Growth brings good things; good things don't bring growth. I believe that internal growth brings about external growth; as within so without.

We live in a world that endorses a bare minimum mentality. We go to school, barely make it to college, get a minimum-wage job, start a family, save for the kids' college, and meanwhile, we are saving for our retirement. We do not strive to become anything or be the best at anything because the society has made it acceptable to settle for anything. But because you are reading this book, you endeavor to hold yourself to a higher standard. The truth is you were born for much more, so start making small adjustments, such as trading off

From Dreaming to Becoming

hours spent watching TV for your own personal growth. It's interesting that we live in a generation that knows *America's Next Top Model* or the next *American Idol* because we want to relate to the contestants and their accomplishments. Today there are many more spin-off shows that duplicate one another because of the success of similar shows. We vote for the winners who are striving to attain their dreams, vicariously wishing we had been the winner. We give others a chance to live their dreams while we are afraid to live our dreams. Who will vote you into living the life of your dreams?

You will never grow and learn new things until you make yourself learn what you don't know. Only then will you realize how much you didn't know when you thought you knew it all. Most people will invest more in a new car or a new house than they will invest in their minds. Your home can be destroyed by fire, your car can be totaled in an accident, but no one can take from you what you're mind possesses. Personal growth is a vital component for realizing your dream. Whether you are an athlete, a politician, or a musician, any dream you have will require a corresponding effort of personal growth on your part. You don't wake up one morning saying, "I am lucky! I won gold medals at the Olympics!" Ask any Olympian and they'll tell you about how hard and long they trained to achieve that gold disc. Some train for years to prepare for this great moment in their lives, others study their opponents and develop skills that give them advantage to win. In the words of Dr. Mike Murdock: "Your significance is not in your similarity from another but in your point of difference from another." You must develop your skills and equip yourself with tools to make your dream a reality by distinguishing yourself. Abraham Lincoln said, "I don't think much of a man who is not wiser than he was yesterday." Life will favor only those who showed up prepared.

The day you stop growing and adding value to yourself is the day you start dying. So take responsibility to invest in your growth. Get a life coach—great coaching increases personal performance. In any discipline, having a coach will embellish your talent and develop your skills. Read great books, study biographies of uncommon achievers, attend great events, listen to motivational and inspiring CDs, DVDs, audio books, or messages. Grow intentionally and strategically to become what you have always dreamed of being. It will cost you time and money, but the results are worthwhile.

When I first started investing in my personal growth through books and tapes, I complained a lot about cost and made excuses that I couldn't afford these expensive resources. I later realized that I couldn't afford *not* to invest in my personal growth if I wanted to make a difference in the world. In his audio CD *Conversations with*

Millionaires, Jim Rohn says, "You have to choose discipline versus regret because discipline weighs ounces and regrets weighs tons." I chose to trade off immediate pleasure for continuous growth, and I purpose to continue my personal growth daily because it's a process not a destination. Continuous personal growth creates an innate ability to develop weaknesses into strengths and cultivate strengths into producing self-discipline, which leads to self-mastery.

> **Continuous personal growth creates an innate ability to develop weaknesses into strengths and cultivate strengths into producing self-discipline, which leads to self-mastery.**

4. Trade Off Saying Yes to Everything for a Categorical No to Some Things

While this seems to be a very simple statement, the implication is profound to your dream. Your dream will not happen when your agenda is full of non-dream-building activities. Most of us grow up thinking that saying no to people is rude. If this is your thinking, you are likely locked into meetings, events, functions, and more, trying to keep up with the popularity contest

The Principle of Tradeoffs

and expectations in your circle of friends. You think by saying yes to everyone else's agendas that it shows your support and solidarity to the group as a team player. But what about your dream to be what you are intended to be? Are these "team players" the same ones who scoff at your dream, saying it's impossible? (Revisit chapter 3.) When it comes to taking care of your dream, you have to learn when to say no to activities and people who do not contribute to positive outcomes to your life or help make your dream a reality.

Not everything that is urgent is important to my dream. I have had to learn to build my life around priorities that are complementary to my dream. Say no to things that don't leverage your dream. One of the hardest things to do is to say no, especially to people you love or care about. Remember that every yes necessitates a no somewhere else in your life, and that no typically translates into putting your dream on the back burner while you help someone else with his or her interests.

Learn to distinguish between what is popular and what is profitable to your dream. People want you to sacrifice your future greatness to get you to share in their compromised present. You have to decide what you permit to grow and increase in your dream environment. You have to be intentional in your decision making by taking an inventory of what brings value to your dream.

Activity does not mean productivity, and just because your itinerary is busy doesn't mean you are efficient and making progress toward your desired dream. You must choose what you want to be ignorant in. It is important to decide what you are willing to live with and what you are unwilling to live without. Don't be a walking warehouse of non-dream-oriented information. That's what the Internet is for. Avoid being a jack-of-all-trades in favor of being a jack-of-specific-trades. In short, eliminate things that sabotage your focus on making your dream a reality. Your only obsession should be your dream. Fix your attention on your dream and don't be a wandering generality. Narrow your attention to information, activity, and people who move you to your dream, not away from it.

5. Trade Off Impatience for Perseverance

Dreams require a lifelong process, which means that we should not expect to experience the results of our efforts until after a time—sometimes a long time. Achieving your dream is not a linear path that can be easily mapped. It's like finding treasure on a mine-infested path; you don't know what to expect. Whenever a farmer plants a seed, he expects the seed to go through a process of growth. The seed has to penetrate the obstacle of the ground before it can emerge. Once the plant surfaces, it must also confront the adversarial conditions of its environment, which include life-choking weeds, the scorching sun, high winds, and drenching rains. So it is with working your dream. It has to be tended to, protected, manipulated, shored up, and more.

In this culture we do not understand the concept of long-suffering. The idea that one has to withstand hardship or difficulty is foreign. As a dreamer, you do well to prepare yourself, because life will throw hardships and disappointments at you. We cannot be hasty or impatient with our dreams. The rewards for those who persevere far exceed the pain that precedes the victory. Are you willing to hang on to your dreams no matter what? As we mention earlier, obstacles are sure to arise, but you can rise above them. It's a choice only you can make. You cannot experience full success with halfhearted commitment. The level of your distinction as a dreamer is predicated on your total commitment.

> **You cannot experience full success with half-hearted commitment. The level of your distinction as a dreamer is predicated on your total commitment.**

Perhaps you are asking yourself, "Why should I prepare to suffer?" Most recently in 2009 our family experienced a very challenging and trying time. We got hit with an unexpected event, something we'd never planned for. One evening my mother-in-law started having chest pains and had to be rushed to the hospital. On the way to the hospital she suffered a massive heart attack and nearly died. The paramedics resuscitated her. After a series of tests, the doctors concluded that my mother-in-law required triple by-pass surgery. Apparently on the day of the surgery the doctors had to take pictures using an endoscopic procedure. As they performed the procedure, my mother-in-law began to bleed internally. The doctors decided to postpone the surgery and do further tests. It turned out that the endoscopic procedure ruptured a tumor lodged in her esophagus. What started as a heart attack led to the discovery of a stage four esophageal cancer. The doctors started chemotherapy, a long, laborious treatment in the fight against cancer. This was a life-altering situation. At the same time my sister-in-law was expecting her first baby, so my mother-in-law was looking forward to be a grandmother, a dream most parents look forward to. However, now she had to deal with the negative reality that threatened her dream. At the same time while undergoing treatment for chemotherapy, the doctors also diagnosed her with end stage renal disease, which meant that she was put on dialysis three times a week. Although the doctors had given her a few weeks to live, she was strong and persevered through the treatment and the pain that she had to endure. I remember seeing her intubated and fighting for her life and her dream.

This illness took a toll on all our lives, emotionally and physically for over a year. Through this entire process my mother-in- law was healed of cancer and lived to see the birth of three of her grandchildren. My mother-in-law is perhaps the best example of long-suffering and perseverance. She refused to capitulate to the challenges that life presented her. She fought courageously and believed that she would live to see her grandchildren. Recently she spent a day with my daughter, her third grandchild since she overcame her illness.

> **You will never outgrow life's challenges; you must simply learn to overcome them.**

Just like my mother-in-law, you may have been confronted by an obstacle such us a major illness, but always keep your dream before you. You will never outgrow life's challenges; you must simply learn to overcome them. Learn to endure hardships if you want to enjoy the triumphs of your dream. As you build on your dream, understand that you will need perseverance, because there will always be difficulties to conquer.

DREAM AXIOMS

- We first have to do what we don't want to do, so we can enjoy second what we want.

- Trade-off is the price you pay to maintain focus on the journey from dreaming to becoming.

- Don't be pigeonholed to sit at the seat of mediocrity because you want to relate to people in your past.

- Whenever you declare your dream, you proclaim a season of adversity, so expect and welcome opposition.

- Don't seek endorsement from people who have not sailed the seas you are pioneering.

- Allow yourself to go through the process, because the process is as important as the promise; don't miss the process.

- Internal growth brings about external growth; as within so without.

- Dreamers are willing to forsake present gratification to pursue their dreams for the joy of future fulfillment.

- Invest your time and resources to attain your most desired dream.

The Principle of Tradeoffs

- Personal growth is a vital component for realizing your dream.

- Your dream will not happen when your agenda is full of non-dream-building activities.

- Learn to distinguish between what is popular and what is profitable to your dream.

- You have to be intentional in your decision making by taking an inventory of what brings value to your dream.

- Achieving your dream is not a linear path that can be easily mapped.

- You cannot experience full success with half-hearted commitment. The level of your distinction as a dreamer is predicated on your total commitment.

Chapter 8

THE PRINCIPLE OF ASSESSMENT

True genius resides in the capacity for evaluation of uncertain, hazardous, and conflicting information.

        Winston Churchill

You've probably heard the definition of insanity is doing the same thing over and over again while expecting different results. Most average dreamers live in a fantasy world where they sit around waiting for opportunities to fall into their laps. We have talked about the necessity of having a plan, because without a plan it's impossible to measure progress, determine any levels of success, or implement necessary corrective actions.

  Those who move from dreaming to becoming constantly evaluate their dreams. It is important to take periodic timeouts to analyze the plan, measure progress,

The Principle of Assessment

identify problems, and then replace underperforming actions with alternatives that function better. Most people never reevaluate their game plans. They start out on a course, but because of complacency or lack of assessment, they demand very little from their efforts. Those who move from dreaming to becoming ask questions that measure progress. Every dream requires continuous evaluation. Assessing your dream allows you to avoid activities that waste time and resources that do not produce a profitable outcome.

> **You cannot build a productive strategy for your dream based on antiquated rules; the rules of the game are constantly changing and so should your strategy.**

The principle of assessment will require that you ask, "What am I doing that is not producing the results I desire?" Every game has a halftime, during which, the coach may change the strategy if the team is not producing the desired results. The team might have started the game applying the coach's strategy but shifted to playing by the rules of the opponent. The coach will reposition the players as well as adjust the strategy to win the game. The objective is not to change the goal of winning but to change the strategy for winning. The

From Dreaming to Becoming

ultimate goal is to become our dream, and this is what winning is about for a dreamer. So during your "half-time," review your progress, reposition your priorities, and replace what is not working.

Most of us start out dreaming, but life's challenges force us to detour and start playing by the rules of our present circumstances. You should not alter the plan to pursue your dreams or have it influenced by your current circumstance. Set your heart on living the life of your dreams.

Assess the Relevance of Your Dream

The principle of assessment allows you to check the relevance of your dream. This may be hard to take, but it's true: let go of dreams that are no longer exciting or relevant. Too many people try to hold on to something way too long in life. There was a time carrying a boom box was exciting and was fashionable. To insist on carrying the boom box in an iPod age is simply ridiculous. We live in an advanced technological world where twelve-year-olds create apps and four-year-olds easily operate computers. Nothing is more powerful as an idea whose timing has come. On the contrary, the reverse can be said of an idea whose timing has passed. You cannot build a productive strategy for your dream based on antiquated rules; the rules of the game are constantly changing and so should your strategy. Stop insisting on fulfilling your "boom box dream" in an iPod generation. Your dream must be relevant.

> *You must either modify your dreams or magnify your skills.*
>
> Jim Rohn

Past successes are only launching pads for overcoming present obstacles and should never be turned into a monument that makes your success a historical event for continuous celebration.

Assess How You View Success

The principle of assessment enables you to assess past successes. It's okay to savor past and present victories, to celebrate and enjoy your successes. Celebrate milestone successes, but don't dwell too much on yesterday's success. The greatest detriment to your future success is your past victories. Past successes are only launching pads for overcoming present obstacles and should never be turned into a monument that makes your success a historical event for continuous celebration. Dreamers store a collection of their past victories because past victories harnessed their strength for future battles. Dreamers constantly draw strength and strategy from past victories. Dreamers treasure the victory of the moment but don't dwell on it, because they have a future to attain. Instead of remaining fixated on what you have accomplished today, let the present victory spur you forward, creating in you a desire for more challenges and greater excitement for other discoveries.

> *Success is going from failure to failure without loss of enthusiasm.*
> Winston Churchill

A true dreamer overcomes complacency by anticipating that "I must be and do more today than I was and did yesterday." Ray Kroc puts it this way: "As long as you are green, you are growing; as soon as you're ripe you start to rot." I believe that most people sabotage their progress by celebrating their achievements too long. Your dream requires small victories along the way. Celebrate but move on to the next challenge.

Assess How You View Failure

John Maxwell's premise in *Failing Forward* is that the difference between average people and successful people is their perception of and response to failure. How you see failure and deal with it impact every aspect of your life. Most people today are afraid to pursue their dreams because they are afraid to fail. So we play it safe and avoid pursuing our dreams, because if we go for it and fail, people will laugh at us or society will call us a failure, and we just can't face that. In fact, most people won't even share their dreams for this very reason.

> **When your heart is set on succeeding only, then an ounce of determination will trounce a ton of failure.**

"What if I share my dream and it never comes to pass?" When your heart is set on succeeding only, then an ounce of determination will trounce a ton of failure. Those who move from dreaming to becoming recognize failure as a challenge to overcome, but they never define their existence and significance from the outcomes of their failure. They learn to say good-bye to yesterday's failure and embrace today's challenges. Failure is not a single event but a process. Just because you tried something and it did not work the first time doesn't make you a failure. The greatest determinant between people who fail and those who succeed is wrapped within their decisions and habits. Judging isolated situations of your life and branding yourself as a failure is an inability to discern greatness when in its presence. Decide that you will succeed no matter what comes your way, and then pattern a consistent habit that will support that decision.

> **Make failure an occasional visitor and not a permanent resident in your lifestyle.**

Most inventors tried numerous times and failed before their ideas became working realities, but they never gave up. Each failure showed them what didn't work and set them on the path to discover what does work. They developed a habit to keep trying because failure is not ultimate. Make failure an occasional visitor and not a permanent resident in your lifestyle.

Failure is only the opportunity to more intelligently begin again.
— Henry Ford

Don't be afraid of failure. Failure is inevitable; everyone fails at some point in life. You cannot always win but you must always learn from your failure in order to win. The weakness of failure is in failing to learn. When you learn to use failure as stepping stones of success, then your deepest failures will become the strongest foundations for your greatest success. In my opinion, the ultimate failure is not to learn from your failures. I believe that failure introduces us to creativity and forces us to search for alternatives. The path for uncommon achievement travels through the land of failure.

> **Failure is inevitable; everyone fails at some point in life. You cannot always win but you must always learn from your failure in order to win. The weakness of failure is in failing to learn.**

Failure is the condiment that gives success its flavor.

Truman Capote

DREAM AXIOMS

- Every dream requires continuous evaluation.

- Assessing your dream allows you to avoid activities that do not produce a profitable outcome.

- You cannot build a productive strategy for your dream based on antiquated rules; the rules of the game are constantly changing and so should your strategy.

- The greatest detriment to your future success is your past victories.

- Past successes are only launching pads for overcoming present obstacles and should never be turned into a monument that makes our success a historical event for continuous celebration.

- Dreamers store a collection of their past victories, because past victories harnessed their strength for future battles.

- Dreamers treasure the victory of the moment but don't dwell on it, because they have a future to attain.

- When your heart is set on succeeding only, then an ounce of determination will trounce a ton of failure.

The Principle of Assessment

- Judging isolated situations of your life and branding yourself as a failure is an inability to discern greatness when in its presence.

- Make failure an occasional visitor and not a permanent resident in your lifestyle.

- Failure is inevitable; everyone fails at some point in life. You cannot always win, but you must always learn from your failure in order to win.

- When you learn to use failure as stepping stones of success, then your deepest failures will become the strongest foundations for your greatest success.

Chapter 9

THE PRINCIPLE OF FAITH

Faith makes us sure of what we hope for and gives us proof of what we cannot see.

Hebrews 11:1 (CEV)

The African impala is incomparable to other jungle animals when it comes to its ability to jump. The impala can jump fifteen feet high and thirty feet long while it exists in its natural habitat in the wild; however, if you take the same animal and confine it behind a four-foot wall in a zoo, the impala would be trapped. Despite its natural, God-given ability to leap over a four-foot wall, the impala will only use its exceptional abilities when it can see where its feet will land. Just like the impala, most of us are trapped in our own prisons of fear, afraid to step out and pursue our dreams because we face too many unknowns. We think, "What if I start then fail?" or "What if I lose all my money?" or "What if it doesn't work?" The truth is we will not know the answers to these questions if we never try. We must have more faith than fear.

It is impossible to make significant strides or enjoy great accomplishments without faith. Great dreamers are also men and women of great faith. When you study the lives of successful people, you will find that there is a great correlation between uncommon achievers and their spiritual lives. In fact, to please God we must have faith—faith in His existence and His ability to reward our quest for Him. Our dreams are inspired by God to help us live our future.

> **Faith counteracts logic; it defies reason through believing in the reality of the unseen before it's a physical reality.**

For our discussion, faith entails the ability to see tomorrow today. Faith gives possibility to that which you are expecting, and births hope for the unseen dream. Faith constitutes believing and speaking with great expectation, the existence of what has not yet manifested to your natural senses. Faith counteracts logic; it defies reason through believing in the reality of the unseen before it's a physical reality.

What kind of faith is this?

- "Believing in advance in something that will only seem logical when seen in reverse." Philip Yancey
- "Faith is to believe what you do not see; the reward for this faith is to see what you believe." St. Augustine
- "Faith is the ability to trust what we cannot see, and with faith we are freed from the flimsy enclosures of life that fear allows to entrap us." Unknown

> True dreamers focus on the results instead of being discouraged by the process.

Faith is not just a mental assent of what you believe; it is the surety of the here and now of your dreams. Most achievers are persuaded about attaining their dreams. To them it's not a question of if but when. True dreamers focus on the results instead of being discouraged by the process. Those who move from dreaming to becoming don't have the word *impossible* in their vocabularies. Faith requires that you see your dream already in existence today—not someday in the future but now. Faith enables us to accomplish what we said we would accomplish, to go through the toughest moments of weariness and fear; yet with courage to stand on hope, even when the course is uncertain. Faith means being willing to live with uncertainties and unknowns.

> *Sometimes life hits you in the head with a brick; don't lose faith.*
>
> Steve Jobs

Faith requires that you see your dream already in existence today — not someday in the future but now.

Leap into the Unknown

Those who have realized their dreams initially had a vision and believed that somehow they would get there. Call it belief, intuition, strong feeling, a positive mind-set, or what some call the "secret." But faith is a confident leap into the unknown. It is not a blind leap, but a calculated leap that is accompanied by a total conviction that one will, somehow against all odds, land on his or her dream. Don't be so much afraid of the unknown that you worry over things that might never happen. Psychologists say that human beings worry and fear about things that never come to pass. To move from dreaming to becoming, I learned to step into the unknown with assurance that something great and wonderful will happen to move me closer to my dream.

> *You block your dream when you allow*
> *your fear to grow bigger than your faith.*
> Mary Manin Morrisey

Faith is progressive not passive. Faith never gives up in times of crisis or challenge. Faith stands up for what it expects. Faith never capitulates to the pressure of fear, misery, or hardship. Faith has no limitations, knows no boundaries. Faith presses on one step at a time.

Faith is a confident leap into the unknown.

Fear is the opposite of faith. Both fear and faith have unknown variables as it relates to the future. Whereas the foundation of fear is pessimism, faith's foundation is optimism. Stop spending your time doubting your beliefs and believing in your doubts. Instead of training the mind and mouth to think and say how your dream will *not* work, train your mind to believe why the dream *will* work. Don't ask Why? Ask Why not? I saw a poster that stated "Faith sees the invisible, believes the incredible and receives the impossible." Faith looks beyond the present circumstances of the here and now. Faith looks through the storms of setbacks, obstacles, bankruptcy, rejection, and such, yet sees the fulfillment of the dream. Having faith influences our perception, how we think and act. In his book *Halftime*, Bob Buford wrote, "Faith doesn't deny reason, but it is different than reason. It accepts, as a gift from God, a different set of capacities. Without faith we are spectators to affairs of the heart and soul. With faith we can go on to engage the other two capacities, our rational and emotional senses."[1]

> **Fear is the opposite of faith. Both fear and faith have unknown variables as it relates to the future. Whereas the foundation of fear is pessimism, faith's foundation is optimism.**

Act on It

Faith requires you, the dreamer, to act on what you believe, to move from your safe zone of familiarity and inaction to a faith zone of uncertainty and action. Faith should propel corresponding action at all times; it demands responsibility. Many people talk about their dreams more than they act on them. Suppose you dream of getting money from your bank account. So you head to an ATM and speak about your debit card, how much

From Dreaming to Becoming

money you have in the account, and what you would do with the funds. You could stay there all day, believing and speaking positively about how much money you would have and what you would do with it. It is not until you insert your debit card into the ATM, enter the pass code, and withdraw the money that you will be able to access your funds to do what you want with it.

> **Faith's reward for taking action is that you get to experience the future you've expected.**

Some people are like that. They have faith in their dreams but never take the step to act on what they believe. Once your dream has taken root in your heart and you own the dream, you must put action behind your faith. If you believe in your dream, take corresponding actions that leads you to the fulfillment of your dream. Faith's reward for taking action is that you get to experience the future you've expected. "If you can believe, all things *are* possible to him who believes."[2] Faith pleases God; when God sees us taking steps to make the dream He gave us a reality, He is pleased.

> *God's only pleasure is to be believed;*
> *God's only pain is to be doubted.*
> — Dr. Mike Murdock

Very often when Jesus performed any miracle, He did it in response to someone's faith not their need. Too many people wait on God to move because of their needs, while God is waiting on them to act because of their faith. As a dreamer, to move from dreaming to becoming, you must have faith in your dream and faith in yourself. This comes by owning your dream (see chapter 4). Talk to yourself about becoming the dream until what seemed unreal becomes real to you. Mohammed Ali told us he was the greatest long before he was, and today, he is synonymous with "I am the greatest!"

Declaration of Your Faith

Faith is not only believing but also speaking into existence the future we desire and following through with corresponding action. Words are more important than we may think. A lot of us use words loosely, and our vocabulary influences our perception of reality. We make other people's failed experiences our own personal expectations by accepting people's clichés and other defeating statements. For instance, most people when asked how they are doing will respond, "Same stuff, different day." We live in a negative world and have become conditioned to the negative stimulus. It's easier to talk about recession, unemployment, and failure than positive events happening. Television news will only air controversial or bad news. But why is no one talking about the millionaires who are emerging from the current global crisis, or about the businesses being started and inventions being made?

It is a self-fulfilling prophecy that expecting failure always gives birth to failure. Dreamers don't talk defeat or failure; instead, dreamers are passionate about the future. They are always excited about a goal they intend to accomplish in their near future.

Words that roll off our tongues are incubators of our dreams. Words that we spoke yesterday make life what it is today. So we must start speaking and setting in motion today the kind of life we want tomorrow.

Words are like seeds. Whatever is in a seed must produce after its own kind. Your tongue either makes you or breaks you. Don't use words to describe your situation; use words to alter your situation. I read an article a while ago on famous people's words on dying. John F. Kennedy said upon arriving in Dallas in 1963, "If someone is going to kill me, they will kill me." "Death and life are in the power of the tongue, those who love it will eat its fruit."[3] Understand that our world as well as our faith is influenced by the words we hear and speak. Your dream is no exception to this rule. The talk of failure will inevitably evoke failure in your life.

Take responsibility, let go of the problems of the past, and start to see yourself living in your dreams today. Talk like your dream will happen any day now. Talk yourself into your desired future, prepare for greatness, and prepare to succeed, not fail. Stretch your faith to believe in the supernatural. Protect yourself from anything that feeds doubt into your life, and allow in anyone or anything that births faith in your life. Expect without exception to attain your goal through faith coupled with corresponding actions. Recite past victories to birth courage for future battles. See crisis as opportunity to use your faith. Disconnect from naysayers and complainers who dampen your expectation with negativity.

DREAM AXIOMS

- Great dreamers are also men and women of great faith.

- Faith gives possibility to that which you are expecting, and births hope for the unseen dream.

- Faith counteracts logic; it defies reason through believing in the reality of the unseen before it's a physical reality.

- Faith requires that you see your dream already in existence today — not someday in the future but now.

- Learn to step into the unknown with assurance that something great and wonderful will happen to move you closer to you dream.

- Both fear and faith have unknown variables as it relates to the future. Whereas the foundation of fear is pessimism, faith has its foundation on optimism.

- Faith looks through the storms of setbacks, obstacles, bankruptcy, rejection, and such, yet sees the fulfillment of the dream.

- Faith requires you, the dreamer, to act on what you believe, to move from your safe zone of familiarity and inaction to a faith zone of uncertainty and action.

THE PRINCIPLE OF FAITH

- If you believe in your dream, take corresponding actions that leads you to the fulfillment of your dream.

- Talk to yourself about becoming the dream until what seemed unreal becomes real to you.

Chapter 10

THE PRINCIPLE OF PASSION

Nothing great in the world has ever been accomplished without passion.

George Wilhelm Friedrich Hegel

Why passion? What is so important about passion? Passion is a driving force, the energy behind the accomplishment of any dream. I think of it as the "baking powder that causes the dream to swell." Passion is what completes the ingredient of our dream and compels the attainment of the dream. You can have a dream without passion, but you cannot accomplish your dream without passion. If you are passionate about your dream, you will pursue it at all cost. Passion keeps you hungry and pressing on toward your desired goal. Passion is the inward drive that motivates behavior or action toward a desired end. Passion comes from conviction about the dream. It is your inner need for pursuit that reveals your passion. According to Webster's dictionary, passion expresses a strong predilection for any pursuit. John Maxwell, in *Put Your Dream to a Test*, describes passion as the starting point of all achievement, and no one can achieve anything of any value without the spark of passionate desire. Also, Dr. Mike Murdock, in *Unstoppable Passion*, defines passion as an excessive and uncommon desire. It's when your goal becomes your only obsession.

> *There is no greatness without a passion to be great, whether it's the aspiration of an athlete or an artist, a scientist, a parent, or a businessperson.*
> — Anthony Robbins

You can have a dream without passion, but you cannot accomplish your dream without passion.

Passion births obsession with your dream, and this obsession creates the focus necessary for the attainment of your dream. Passion will always energize you to pursue your dreams despite prevailing circumstances in your life. In the words of Oprah Winfrey, "Passion is energy. Feel the power that comes from focusing on what excites you." What excites you? Are you passionate about it? What do you love to hear about? Does it awaken a desire or pull you to go after it?

> **Passion is the inward drive that motivates behavior or action toward a desired end.**

Desire

Desire is an evidence of passion. What you desire intensely you will pursue relentlessly. You will be passionate only about something you love. A lot of people are trying to birth passion for something that they have no desire to attain. In the words of Robert Allen, "Everything you want is outside of your comfort zone." You have to desire change and be passionate about getting out of your comfort zone. The world will only be changed by men and women with big dreams whose passions are greater, who desire change more than they desire their own comfort and security. You cannot awaken passion for a dream that you do not desire. I remember having a conversation with a young lady who was admiring a car she referred to as her "dream car."

THE PRINCIPLE OF PASSION

During our conversation I told her to go after it; you can have it. All you need is to set a plan in order to have it.

But she said, "I cannot afford it. Do you know how much that car costs? That car is for rich folks." She desired the car but was not willing to pay the price it takes to have it.

About that same time I had an epiphany: most people admire other people's dreams and things, yet they have no passion to pursue or make their own dreams come true. You have to want your dream bad enough that you are willing to pay the price to have it. You might not have it immediately, but if you are truly passionate about it, you will have it. You dream is not a cute idea that you pursue when you feel like it or maybe when you have time. Your dream requires commitment. Commitment is a portrait of passion. When everyone else is tired and backs out, the passionate are just getting started on their journey of pursuit. Passionate people are committed to the completion of their dreams.

> **Desire is an evidence of passion. What you desire intensely you will pursue relentlessly.**

In his book *Self Matters*, Dr. Phil wrote, "If you have no purpose, you have no passion. If you have no passion, you have sold yourself out. I know that, because

From Dreaming to Becoming

I know that within each of us there are passions that, if acknowledged and released, will energize and excite the experiences of life."[1] The apostle Paul had a passion to share his message with the Gentiles with whom he was imprisoned. Paul suffered hunger, was persecuted, experienced shipwrecks, even feared for his life; however, in all these things Paul had a persuasion because of passion to his assignment. "I do not count myself to have apprehended; but one thing *I do*, forgetting those things which are behind and reaching forward to those things which are ahead, I press toward the goal for the prize of the upward call of God in Christ Jesus."[2] It will take uncommon passion to achieve the dream that God has placed in your heart, for without it, your success is restricted. Passionate people are persistent people, and their doggedness eventually leads to success.

> Passion is the flame that lights up the fire in our dreams.

Protect Your Passion

Passion is the fuel that God supplies to achieve the dreams He placed in us. It is the flame that lights the fire in our dreams. Therefore, protect your passion by disconnecting from people who seek to extinguish your passion and dampen your spirit. Pursue people, activities, and environments that fan the flame of your passion. People will pay you to do what you love and are passionate about. Fight ferociously for your passion. Anyone who doesn't share in your passion will not protect what you value, and this will eventually deplete your passion and affect your dreams.

DREAM AXIOMS

- You can have a dream without passion, but you cannot accomplish your dream without passion.

- Passion is the inward drive that motivates behavior or action toward a desired end.

- Passion births obsession with your dream, and obsession creates the focus necessary for the attainment of your dream.

- Passion is the fuel that God supplies to achieve the dreams He placed in us.

- Desire is an evidence of passion. What you desire intensely you will pursue relentlessly.

- You dream is not a cute idea that you pursue when you feel like or maybe when you have time. Your dream requires commitment.

- Commitment is a portrait of passion.

- It will take uncommon passion to achieve the dream that God has placed in your heart, for without it, your success is restricted.

- Anyone who doesn't share in your passion will not protect what you value, and this will eventually deplete your passion and affect your dreams.

Conclusion

Friends, *From Dreaming to Becoming* is not exhaustive on all that necessitates the attainment of our dreams; however, we can take these ten major principles and begin the journey to bringing our dreams to life. These ten principles are ultimate laws that are essential for laying the right foundation and for transitioning your dream from your mind to reality. They are the "Ten Commandments" for every dreamer. My prayer is that you will learn them and implement them so your success will be inevitable.

Don't settle; do not agree with your status quo. How many times do you have to accept your condition and agree with your circumstances instead of fighting back? Will you allow someone else to take your place in history and realize his or her dream while you sit on yours? Not every need has been met, not all inventions have been discovered. Moments are reserved for your genius to emerge. Open your eyes to the unlimited possibilities. You still have a place on earth set aside to create a

From Dreaming to Becoming

historical and generational indelible impact. Ten years ago we knew nothing of Mark Zuckerberg, inventor of Facebook, Internet celebrity Gary Vaynerchuck, *Wine Library TV*, or Timothy Ferris, one of the most innovative business minds in social media, yet they've impacted countless lives and their names will forever be remembered for having pursued their dreams.

The reality is you can continue trying to make a living, but this will always limit your true potential. Millions of people are living the rat race. Many are afraid to take the next step that will lead to their dreams being liberated from the prison house of inaction. Please, do not become a human hamster that is forever busy but never effective, always toiling but has nothing to show for it. Give up the excuses and start pursuing your dreams. You are the miracle you have been waiting for. Recess is over. It's time to turn your dreams into realities.

See you at the top!

NOTES

INTRODUCTION
1. Carl Mays, *Anatomy of a Leader* (Successories Inc., 1997).
2. Andy Stanley, *Visioneering: God's Blueprint for Developing and Maintaining Personal Vision* (Sisters: Multnomah Publishers, Inc., 1999).
3. John C. Maxwell, *Dare to Dream, Then Do It* (Thomas Nelson, 2006).
4. Joel 2:28 (Author's paraphrase.)

CHAPTER 1
1. Napoleon Hill, *Think and Grow Rich* (Arc Manor LLC, 2007).
2. Luke 11:34
3. Mitch Albom, *Tuesdays with Morrie* (Doubleday, 1997).
4. Bob Buford, *Halftime: Changing Your Game Plan from Success to Significance* (Zondervan, 2008).

5. Victor Frankl, *Man's Search for Meaning* (Beacon Press, 2006).
6. Jeremiah 1:5 (Author's paraphrase.)
7. Bishop T. D. Jakes, *Reposition* (Atria, 2008).
8. Phillip C. McGraw, PhD, *Self Matters: Creating Your Life from the Inside Out* (Free Press, 2001).

CHAPTER 2

1. Charles Phillips, *How to Develop a Success Mentality* (Kingdom Publications, 2002).
2. Proverbs 23:7 (Author's paraphrase.)
3. John C. Maxwell. *Dare to Dream.*
4. Philippians 4:8 NIV
5. Proverbs 4:23 CEV
6. Philippians 4:13 (Author's paraphrase.)
7. Denis Waitley, *The Psychology of Winning* (Nightingale Conant, 1997).

CHAPTER 3

1. Bishop T. D. Jakes, *Maximize the Moment: God's Action Plan for Your Life* (G.P. Putnam's Sons, 1999).
2. John 2:24 NKJV
3. Proverbs 11:14
4. Proverbs 27:17

NOTES

CHAPTER 4
1. Genesis 37:19 (Author's paraphrase.)
2. John C. Maxwell, *Put Your Dream to the Test* (Thomas Nelson, 2009).
3. Dr. Mike Murdock, *1001 Wisdom Keys* (Wisdom International, 2009).
4. Carelton "Carly" Fiorina (commencement remarks, MIT graduation, June 2, 2000).
5. Steve Jobs (commencement address, Stanford University graduation, June 12, 2005).
6. Philippians 3:13 NKJV
7. Andy Andrews, *The Traveler's Gift* (Thomas Nelson, 2002).
8. Mark 11:24 (Author's paraphrase.)
9. John C. Maxwell, *Dare to Dream*.

CHAPTER 5
1. Dr. Myles Munroe, *Releasing Your Potential* (Destiny Image, 1992).
2. Ecclesiastes 9:11
3. Proverbs 16:9 NKJV
4. Luke 14:28–31 NKJV
5. David J. Schwartz, *The Magic of Thinking Big* (New York: Prentice Hall, 1997).
6. Flip Flippen, *The Flip Side: Break Free of the Behaviors That Hold You Back* (Springboard Press, 2007).

CHAPTER 6

1. Steve Siebold, *177 Mental Toughness Secrets of the World Class: The Thought Processes, Habits and Philosophies of the Great Ones* (London House, 2005).
2. Andy Andrews, *The Traveler's Gift*.
3. John R. Wooden with Jamison Steve, *Wooden: A Lifetime of Observations and Reflection On and Off the Court* (McGraw-Hill, 1997).

CHAPTER 9

1. Bob Buford, *Halftime: Changing Your Game Plan from Success to Significance* (Zondervan, 2008).
2. Mark 9:23 NKJV
3. Proverbs 18:21 NKJV

CHAPTER 10

1. Phillip C. McGraw, *Self Matters* (Free Press, 2001).
2. Philippians 3:13 NKJV

About the Author

Phinehas Kinuthia is passionate about ordinary people discovering and living a life of purpose through accomplishing their dreams. He is an international speaker, author, educator, life-coach, mentor, leader, and entrepreneur. He earned a Bachelor of Science Degree in Interdisciplinary Studies from University of Houston- Downtown, and he has degrees in Applied Science Real Estate, Business Management, and Religion. His interest in pursuing new opportunities has led him through diverse careers including real estate, insurance sales, small business, and entrepreneurship.

Phinehas's life is a compelling story that embodies his message that anyone can make their dreams a reality. Raised in poverty in Africa, he came to America with only $200 and a vision of unlimited possibility. He is an example that accomplishing dreams is of absolutely possible.

Phinehas is an expert on setting and achieving dreams. In 2010 he started Global Enlightenment

From Dreaming to Becoming

Center, a non-profit organization that impacts local and international communities and schools offering scholarships and support for food banks, orphanages, and domestic violence shelters, while also equipping and developing leaders.

To the disenfranchised, Phinehas is a voice of hope and inspiration through speaking, books, and training. He conducts training workshops and offers programs to help people discover their purpose, and teach them how to pursue their dreams and live a full, passionate life of faith. He has taught people from different walks of life worldwide. His philosophy is that everyone possesses hidden treasure that is valuable only when it is discovered. He believes that you can be more than you are, go farther than you have, and reach higher than you ever thought possible.

Phinehas is available for media appearances and speaking engagements. Learn more about his story and his programs, and be inspired to reach your dreams without limitation.

About the Author

For information on speaking, coaching, seminars,
and workshops contact Phinehas at:

Phinehas K Enterprises
PO Box 6529, Katy, TX 77491
Tel: 1-800-971-8076
Email: info@phinehask.com
www.phinehask.com

Notes

Notes

Notes

Notes

Notes